Contents

1 Who am I?

Recipe for a human being

Somebody has produced a list of ingredients of what is needed to make a human being:

Water: enough to fill a 22-litre barrel (about 10 gallons).

Fat: enough to make seven bars of soap.

Phosphorus: enough to put on the heads of 2,200 matches.

Carbon: enough to fill 9,000 lead pencils.

Iron: enough to make a nail about three centimetres long.

Lime: enough to whitewash a normal-sized hen coop.

But is this all that we are? Is anything missing? The two photographs in this unit seem to give different answers to these questions. The first

A 'crouch' or 'foetal' burial. There was plenty of space in the grave, so why might the body be placed in this position?

shows a victim of the Holocaust: a Jewish man being shot. He is about to fall into a pit where the bodies of many other Jewish men, women and children, and perhaps some gypsies and Jehovah's Witnesses lie. They, too, were victims of the Holocaust, the attempt by Adolf Hitler and his Nazi supporters to kill all the Jews they could lay their hands on. Six million of them died between 1939 and 1945.

All human beings are made up of the same chemicals. People of different skin colours share the same blood groups. Two students studying blood in a science lesson, one black, the other white, were amazed to find that they belonged to the same blood group! One of the Jews Hitler wanted to exterminate could have given him life-saving blood when Hitler was injured in a plot on his life! Underneath our differences in size or colour of skin, and despite our various religious beliefs and political ideas, we human beings are essentially the same.

The second photograph shows a burial which took place more than 2,000 years ago. It shows the body of a woman curled up in a grave. The people who buried her had no need for reading and writing, and so left no writings to tell us what they believed. To some extent we can only guess about their ideas of God (if they believed in one), the meaning of life, and what they believed happened when a person died – whether there was some after-death existence or not. The woman is curled up in what is known as a 'foetal position'. That means it is placed in the earth in the same position as it had lain for nine months in its mother's womb.

A man being shot on the edge of a mass grave. Sometimes these pits are still found in Poland and East Germany

Spirituality
in focus

**Edited by
W Owen Cole**

Charanjit AjitSingh
E Huda Bladon
W Owen Cole
Arye Forta
Dilip Kadodwala
John White
Andrea Willson

Heinemann Educational Publishers
Halley Court, Jordan Hill, Oxford OX2 8EJ
a division of Reed Educational & Professional
Publishing Ltd

OXFORD FLORENCE PRAGUE MADRID ATHENS
MELBOURNE AUCKLAND KUALA LUMPUR
SINGAPORE TOKYO IBADAN NAIROBI KAMPALA
JOHANNESBURG GABORONE
PORTSMOUTH NH (USA) CHICAGO
MEXICO CITY SAO PAULO

First published 1997

00 99 98 97
10 9 8 7 6 5 4 3 2 1

British Library Cataloguing in Publication Data
A catalogue record for this book is available from the
British Library

ISBN 0 435 30245 0

Designed and typeset by Dennis Fairey & Associates
Printed and bound in Spain by Mateu Cromo

Acknowledgements

The publishers would like to thank the following for permission to reproduce copyright material:
Amana Publications for the verses from *The Meaning of the Holy Qur'an*, new edition with revised translation and commentary by Abdullah Yusuf Ali, courtesy of Amana Publications, Beltsville, Maryland, USA, in the Islam section of this book; Sydney Carter © 1963 Stainer & Bell Ltd, London, England for the lines from 'Lord of the Dance' on p. 48; material from *The Alternative Service Book* 1980 is copyright © The Central Board of Finance of the Church of England and is reproduced by permission, on p. 41; excerpts from *The Jewish Way in Death & Mourning* by Maurice Lamm. Copyright © 1969. Reprinted by arrangement with Jonathan David Publishers Inc, Middle Village, New York 11379, on p. 92; J M Dent and Sons Ltd for the extracts from *Hindu Scriptures* translated by R C Zaehner, 1966, on pp. 54, 55, 56, 57, 60; the poem 'Silent God' by Edwina Gateley is used with permission of Anthony Clarke Publishers, on p. 53; *The Guardian* for the quotes taken from 'And when I die, don't send me flowers' by Gary Younge, 25/5/96, on pp. 120–1; David Higham Associates for the lines from 'The force that through the green fuse drives the flower' by Dylan Thomas, published by J M Dent and Sons Ltd, on p. 22; Hodder Headline for the extract from *The Ascent of Everest* by John Hunt, reproduced by permission of Hodder & Stoughton Ltd/New English Library Ltd, on p. 24; The Humanist Association for the logo on p. 20; extract from *To Kill a Mockingbird* by Harper Lee, published by William Heinemann Ltd, reproduced by permission of Reed Books on p. 21; Laurie Lee for the extract from *The First Born*, reprinted by permission of the Peters Fraser & Dunlop Group Ltd on pp. 16–17; Memory Lane Music for the lines from the song 'What a wonderful world' on p. 22. Copyright © 1967 renewed 1995. Renewal copyright assigned to Ailene Music Inc. and Range Road Music Inc. and Quartet Music Inc. Rights for the world outside the United States and Canada administered by Memory Lane Music Limited, London, Carlin Music Corp., London, and Muziekuitgeverij Artemis BV, Naarden, Holland. International copyright secured. All rights reserved. 'What a wonderful world' words and music by Bob Thiele and George D Weiss © 1967 by Range Road Music Inc., Quartet Music Co. Inc. and Abiline Music Inc. Lyric reproduction by permission of Carlin Music Corp – UK administrator – on p. 22; Mesorah Publications, Brooklyn, NY for the extracts from *Anatomy of a Search* by A Tatz, 1987, on p. 87, and from *The Call of the Torah* by E Munk, 1994, on p. 88, reprinted with permission of Art Scroll/Mesorah; Navajivan Trust for the quotes by Mahatma Gandhi on pp. 9, 61; OUP for the extracts from the *Bhagavad Gita* as translated by R C Zaehner, 1969, used by permission of Oxford University Press on pp. 56, 59, 60, 63; © Oxford University Press and Cambridge University Press for the extracts from *The Revised English Bible* in the Christianity section of this book; Penguin Books Ltd for the extracts from *Buddhist Scriptures* by Edward Conze, Penguin Classics, 1971, on p. 32,

from *The Upanishads* as translated by J Mascaro, 1965, on pp. 57 and 67, and from the *Bhagavad Gita* as translated by J Mascaro, 1962, on p. 63; Prentice Hall Inc. for the extract from *American Judaism: Adventure in modernity* by Jacob Neusner, © 1972. Reprinted by permission of Prentice Hall Inc, Upper Saddle River, NJ, on p. 94; Quartet Books for the extract from *98 Not Out* by Fenner Brockway on pp. 12, 22; W Rahula for the extract from *What the Buddha Taught*, 1990, with permission of the publisher Grove Press, USA on p. 39; Random House UK Limited for the poem 'An ordinary day' by Norman MacCaig, published by Chatto & Windus, on p. 23; Routledge Ltd for the extracts from *New Hopes for a Changing World* by Bertrand Russell, Allen & Unwin, 1951 on p. 19 and *The Life of the Buddha* by Edward J Thomas, RKP, 1975 on pp. 28, 38; Simon & Schuster for the extracts from *Teshuva: A guide for the newly observant Jew* by Rabbi Adin Steinsaltz. Translated and edited by Michael Swirsky. Copyright © 1982 by The Domino Press, Jerusalem. Translation copyright © 1987 by The Free Press, a division of Simon & Schuster. Reprinted with permission of the publisher, on p. 83; SPCK for the prayers from *The Prayers of African Religions* by John S Mbiti, SPCK, 1975, used by permission of the publishers, on pp. 116–17; Weidenfeld and Nicolson for the extract from *Jerusalem* by T Kollek and M Pearlman, 1968, on pp. 84–5; © Wally Whyton, Durham Music Ltd, 11 Uxbridge St, London W8 7TQ for the lines from 'Leave them a flower' on p. 23; Wisdom Publications, 361 Newbury Street, Boston, USA for the quotes by Joel Levey and Tarthang Tulku from *The Fine Arts of Relaxation, Concentration and Meditation* on pp. 33, and the extract from *Introduction to Tantra* by Lama Yeshe on p. 39.

The publishers would like to thank the following for permission to use photographs:
Abbas/Magnum p. 11; Charanjit AjitSingh pp. 98, 100, 101; Allsport p. 25 (bottom); Ancient Art and Architecture p. 67 (left); Associated Press/Topham Picture Point p. 21; Siân R Baker p. 118 (both); Robin Bath pp. 27, 30, 34 (bottom left and right), 37; British Library/Bridgeman Art Library p. 44; Chris Caldicott/Still Pictures p. 66 (bottom); Camera Press p. 4 (top); J Allan Cash p. 93, 114; Circa Photo Library p. 48; Douglas Dickens p. 58; M Izzi Dien p. 80; CM Dixon p. 4 (top); Mark Edwards/Still Pictures pp. 13, 55; Elliot Erwitt/Magnum Photos p. 16; Mary Evans Picture Library pp. 19, 25 (top), 62; William Fautre/Still Pictures p. 12; Findhorn Foundation p. 123; John Fryer/Circa Photo Library p. 51 (left); Sally and Richard Greenhill pp. 17, 89 (top and middle); J Haocett/Panos Pictures p. 107; Michael Holford p. 54; William Holtby/Circa p. 31; Chris Honeywell p. 67 (right); Rebecca Hossack Gallery p. 115; Hulton Getty p. 61; Humanist Association p. 20 (logo); ILEA p. 22 (bottom); Jan Paul Kool p. 36; Justin Leighton/Network p. 9; Library Committee of the Religious Society of Friends of Britain p. 49; Georges Lopez/Still Pictures p. 22 (top); Mansell Collection p. 18 (bottom); Carlos Reyes Manzo/Andes Press Agency pp. 28, 43, 46, 47, 50, 51 (right), 82, 89 (bottom); Roland and Sabrina Michaud/John Hillelson p. 72; Bipin J Mistry p. 56; Bipin J Mistry/Circa Photo Library p. 106 (top); NASA/Science Photo Library p. 122; Novovitch–Liaison/Gamma/Frank Spooner Pictures p. 24 (right); Claude Nuridsany and Marie Perennou/Science Photo Library p. 95; Jonathan Olley/Network p. 7; Ben Osborne/BBC Natural History Unit p. 15; Ann and Bury Peerless p. 66 (top), 110; Punjab and Sind Bank pp. 97, 103; Zev Radovan pp. 85, 91 (bottom); Raghu Rai/Magnum p. 65; Christopher Rennie/Robert Harding Picture Library p. 112; R Rutman p. 91 (top); HS Sagoo pp. 104 (both), 105, 106 (both), 107 (both), 109 (both); Peter Sanders pp. 68, 69, 70, 71, 74, 75, 76, 77, 78, 79, 81; Sean Smith/*The Guardian* p. 120; Society for the Propagation of the Gospel pp. 41, 45; Jean-Michel Turpin/Gamma/Frank Spooner Pictures p. 20 (top); Twin Studio/Circa Photo Library p. 108; Tom Van Sant/Science Photo Library p. 14; Andy Weber pp. 26, 32, 34 (top), 38; John White p. 18 (top); K Yamada/Chris Bonnington Picture Library p. 24 (left); Zefa Pictures p. 87.

Cover photograph by Robert Harding/Sharpshooters.

The publishers have made every effort to trace copyright holders. However, if any material has been incorrectly acknowledged, we would be pleased to correct this at the earliest opportunity.

Authors' acknowledgements

Charanjit AjitSingh would like to thank Dr Owen Cole and also her family for their support and comments. E Huda Bladon would like to thank M Izzi Dien. Dilip Kadodwala would like to thank Vilash for her help and support. Andrea Willson would like to thank Lama Zopa Rimpoche, Dr David Stott, Owen Cole, Andy Weber and her Buddhist friends who contributed their thoughts and opinions mentioned throughout the text. John White thanks Dr James Hemming and his other colleagues on the British Humanist Association's Education Committee.

The preparation of this book coincided with a long bout of pneumonia. This meant that I had to rely upon the kindness of many people. First among these are the editorial team at Heinemann. I must also thank my co-authors for their patience and thoroughness in writing the sections with the minimum of guidance by the editor. Several people must be thanked by name. Suzanne Wright of the Chichester Institute of Higher Education library unhesitatingly searched for information. Eluned Lyons, Siân and Mark Baker provided material on the Australian Aborigines and Native Americans. During my illness I was constantly reminded of the support of friends. Their encouragement was of immense value. Finally, I have always owed a debt to my wife, Gwynneth, that I can never hope to repay. At no time has my need for her tender loving care been greater; it has never been so generously given – and she found time to read the proofs! – W Owen Cole

Perhaps that gives a clue to any beliefs which they might have had. It might suggest how they regarded the earth.

The chemical ingredients for making a human being and the two photographs tell us that there are several different views on what a human being is. What matters is which views we think are acceptable, and which we think should be rejected.

Does language matter?

It may even make a difference which words we use to describe people. A person who is responsible for finding the homeless somewhere to live could describe them as 'casualties of human indifference'. Unemployed teenagers could be 'layabouts and scroungers', or 'young school leavers in need of help'. The blacks who were taken into slavery 250 years ago were sometimes called 'savages'. That name enabled white slavers to take them from Africa to America without any qualms of conscience because they did not regard them as human beings but as wild, savage animals. 'Senior citizen' may give people who have worked a long time for family and society a sense that they still matter. 'Old age pensioner' might suggest that they are a costly nuisance to society, ready for the scrap heap. Some Native Americans and Australian Aborigines call the old 'elders' or maybe the wise ones'.

Returning to our chemical formula for a human being, a story is told of a speaker at Hyde Park Corner, the place where people with a message stand on Sunday afternoons, shouting their ideas to anyone who will listen to them. The man was trying to tell people that there was really nothing worth living for. He might have read the formula, because he was telling listeners that they were nothing but phosphorous and glue! A young couple passed. The woman was holding her tiny baby in her arms. She looked at the baby, then at her husband and said: 'Phosphorous and glue, Harry, he doesn't know the half of it!'

Understanding the views of others

Still, the man had a point of view and we should try to understand the ideas, values and beliefs of different people. That is what this book is about. The women and men who have written it are not trying to persuade anyone that their beliefs are right and those of other people are wrong. What the book is asking you to do is to think, and then, if you wish, to make up your own mind whether human beings are spiritual or not, and whether, in fact, there is such a thing as spirituality. You have, at least, a right to learn about some of the ideas which exist around you and which, in the case of the Australian Aborigines, for example, are older than anything but the hills, valleys and rivers in the country in which you live; much older than any of the structures which human beings have built: perhaps 40,000 years old.

The puzzle of life is probably as old as life itself. Some men and women of wisdom claim to have solved it, but life isn't like doing mathematics: there are no answers which can be proved – only answers that make sense to us (and perhaps others that do not). But there are men and women who say: 'I want to learn about your truth as well as my truth, because the more I know, the wiser I can become'.

Tasks

1   What do you think the followers of Adolf Hitler thought about the Jews they wanted to kill?

2   What thoughts do you think the family had as they dug the grave and laid someone in it? How did they feel as they covered the grave with soil? What do you think the family hoped? Does the burial necessarily suggest that the family had religious beliefs? Does it prove that they believed in life beyond death?

3   Create a discussion between the man who shot the Jew and the parents of the dead woman about the value of a life.

2 | Faith

Is it true?

This is a very important question. We often ask it and the answer isn't always as easy and clear as we would like it to be. Here are a few examples:

- Is it true that England won the soccer World Cup at Wembley in 1966?

- Is it true that the sun rises in the east?

- Is it true that the earth is a friendly place?

- Is it true that there is a God?

Yes, England did win the World Cup in 1966! It is possible to see the film of Geoff Hurst scoring the winning goal and of Bobby Moore being awarded the trophy. Accounts of the match can be given by Bobby and Jack Charlton and are written in the newspapers in libraries. Of course, there may be people who will not accept this evidence. But it is generally accepted as a fact that can be proved.

Most of you are likely to agree that the sun rises in the east. On a good day, if we get up early enough, we can see it for ourselves. But is this really true? Does the sun actually *rise* at all? Doesn't the earth rotate in such a way that the sun *seems* to rise? Scientists might use the language of everyday life, but they know that the sun doesn't rise or set.

What do we mean by asking whether the earth is friendly or not? If we slip or are tackled heavily at rugby in September, before the ground has become muddy, we won't think that it is very friendly. It hurts us! But if we look at things in a different way we might say that it *is* friendly, because it supports life, in the way that the moon and sun and other planets do not seem to. We can look at the evidence in two ways and arrive at different conclusions, perhaps because of what we believe.

For well over 2,000 years, ever since human beings could write down their thoughts, it is clear that they have argued about the existence of God. One person can look at rocks being lashed by the sea, or the moon and stars on a clear night, or a sleeping baby, or enjoy the scent of a rose and say: 'There must be a God'. Another may conclude that there is not: that the flower's scent is merely there to attract bees and other insects for the purpose of pollination, or that reaction to the baby is a human instinct.

The answers to the biggest questions of life don't lie in proof but in faith. No one can prove that there is a God, or that there is not one; or that life has a purpose. We can be agnostic, which means saying 'I don't know', or we can say that we don't care, but otherwise we are talking about belief. Scientists may argue about whether God exists or not, but in matters of belief they know no more than anyone else.

Faith

Faith goes through a number of stages. When we were small children we probably believed in Santa Claus. Now we don't. Or do we? Can Santa Claus be a metaphor, a way of expressing a series of beliefs? If I say I believe in him it might mean that I believe in the spirit which he represents: in kindness, in giving, in being generous. When we were small children we probably believed that we were the centre of the universe. All we had to do was to wish and we would have whatever we wanted. As we become mature we realise that we are not alone. If I join a sports club and wish to win the high jump, I have to train and practise – and I might still lose. What if I do? Can I find happiness and meaning in knowing that I did my best and was beaten by someone better? Or do I sulk and lose heart? Can I change my faith from believing that I am the best, to accepting defeat but being satisfied in taking part, and maybe in being amazed at what human beings can achieve?

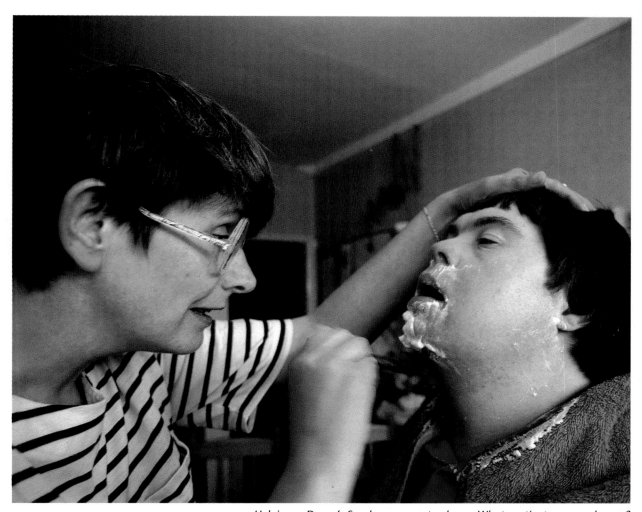

Helping a Down's Syndrome man to shave. What motivates a good carer?

Faith is related to experience. We may trust people until someone lets us down badly. Then we may say: 'I'll never trust anyone again'. A week or so later someone we scarcely know may take the trouble to help us, and our faith in human nature may be restored.

Love

The greatest act of faith that most human beings ever make is to love someone. We begin by loving ourselves and expecting parents, grandparents, sisters and brothers to put us at the centre of their universe. (If they don't we can always throw a tantrum at the supermarket checkout!) As we grow up we may discover that we can't always get what we want, but Mum loves us all the same. We may even find ourselves giving love to others, not to get something from them, but just because we love them. This is altruism: giving without wish for reward. It is probably the most mature act of faith of which we are capable: believing and acting without wanting anything in return.

Tasks

1   What are the differences between proof and belief?

2   Why do some people say that the most important things in life are related to faith?

3   Discuss the view that it is possible to have faith without believing in God.

3 Conscience

Prudence

Watch a toddler taking a toy that her little sister is playing with. She looks carefully and, if no one is looking, pounces and takes it. This is the beginning of conscience – and may be the end of its development. Many people seem to think that the difference between right and wrong is whether they can get away with it. The kind of behaviour that depends on whether someone is watching and whether the grown-ups approve is called 'prudential'. It is prudent, wise, sensible not to upset those who are more powerful than ourselves.

Are human beings like animals?

Human beings seem to be the only creatures who have consciences. Of course, if we observe animals – a pet cat, for example – we may see them behave like human toddlers. A cat might be tempted to leap on to the table to steal a piece of fish, but it knows what reaction to expect, so it doesn't. It may stalk a bird in the garden until it sees its owner watching disapprovingly; then it will stop, looking angry or rather sheepish, wagging its tail in annoyance. This may not be because it knows that what it is doing is wrong, but because it knows that we disapprove. Family pets behave as we have trained them to behave. Hunting birds is an instinctive activity for cats: when stalking them they are behaving according to their nature.

There may not be much difference between little human beings and animals, but when children reach the age of fourteen the law says that they are old enough to know the difference between right and wrong and can be punished for any criminal acts which they commit. It says that they have developed enough to behave 'properly' – whether someone is watching or not.

Is obeying the law all that matters?

Society decides what is legally right and wrong. Most of us accept the decisions of the community and keep the law. If the law says that we must go to school until we are sixteen years old, most of us go without question. If it says we must pay income tax (if we are fortunate enough to have a job), we do. When it was said that it was lawful to own slaves, many people who could afford to possess them were slave owners. When the law was changed they obeyed it and slaves were given their freedom.

However, sometimes men and women are guided by a sense of right and wrong that doesn't depend on the law. For example, there were Americans and Europeans, including Britons, who said that slavery was wrong in principle, long before the law was changed. In fact they were the people who struggled to have slavery abolished. There have been others

'But I'm only obeying my instincts!'

Protesters opposing the legal export of live animals

who denounced racism in South Africa during the years of apartheid. This was a period of the separate development of blacks and whites, in which the blacks came off worse and were subject to discrimination, enduring inferior schooling, medical care and housing, for example. In Britain, when a law was passed compelling men to join the armed forces in World War I, some men opposed it, claiming that killing other human beings, even in war time, was wrong. They were sent to prison.

While many people keep the law because they are afraid to be caught, there are others who obey it because breaking it infringes the rights of others. They do not mug old ladies because they respect other people on principle, even if they have never met them before. They believe they have no right to harm anyone else's person or to take their property.

More than law?

Some people say there is a higher law, and that something inside us is aware of a level of truth which is more than conventional and more than what society requires of us. This view has inspired some of the world's greatest humanitarians. One of them, an Indian named Gandhi, believed that all faiths and races should live together peacefully. A member of his own religion felt that he was being a traitor to it, and shot him.

One of Gandhi's principles, which guided his conscience and which he suggested politicians should follow, was:

'Recall the face of the poorest and most helpless person you may have seen and ask yourself if the step you contemplate is going to be of any use to him. Will he gain anything by it? Will it restore him to control over his life and destiny?'

Tasks

1. Is there such a thing as conscience or is it simply being scared of what our mates or parents might say or what the law might do to us?

2. What things in our lives can help us develop our consciences if we believe that we have one?

3. Discuss the view that it doesn't matter what we do so long as we hurt no one but ourselves.

4. Does having a conscience suggest that we are more than creatures of instinct like dogs or cats? Give reasons for your answer.

4 The spiritual search

St Augustine once said:

> 'Our hearts are not at rest until they rest in you.'

There is plenty of evidence of restlessness which makes great men and women or rich ones dissatisfied with life. Sports people, film stars and TV personalities can all find life too much for them.

Making choices

Human beings can and do make choices. Life is full of decisions and parents, other relatives, careers advisers, friends, youth club leaders and a host of other people seek to help us make them. Choices may include which GCSEs to take, which jobs to go for, whether to stay on into the sixth form, whether to go to FE college or university. Then there is the matter of choosing a life partner.

Sometimes choices are easy but painful – like those for the sons of Welsh or Durham miners who, until the 1960s or '70s, had only life in the pit to look forward to. Dad, brothers, uncles, granddads had all been coal miners; there seemed to be no other life. It was the same story at the mills of Lancashire, Yorkshire, and parts of Scotland. Even choosing a husband or wife was fairly uncomplicated. It was often someone from the same town, who lived in the next street, who went to the same school. Maybe this is less often the case now than in our grandparents' time. Travel has changed many aspects of life. At college a white European might fall in love with a black South African, or a Spanish American. It might still be unlikely for an inhabitant of the Equatorial rain forest or the Amazon to meet an Inuit from the Tundra and fall in love – but it cannot be ruled out. Of course, some of us never leave our home towns, but today many people have to leave to look for work.

Faith choices

Most of us are very traditional in many ways. When we leave home we may use the same toothpaste as our parents, or prefer the pizzas or hamburgers they introduced us to. This is often true of religion, as well. If our parents belong to no church we probably will not, either. If they are Catholics, we are likely to be, too, though we may drop out. Not many of us are likely to change our religion altogether, from Jew to Buddhist or from Sikh to Christian – but some people do.

Here are the recollections of two people who decided to change from one religion to another:

'My life seemed to be going nowhere. At eighteen I left home because there was no work where I lived and I was fed up sponging off my parents. Oh, they didn't mind. They didn't see it that way, but I did. I went to Birmingham, about 30 miles away. There should be plenty that I could do there. I'd got 'O' levels in Maths and English and was ready to try anything. I couldn't find a job, but I did manage to get a room in a hostel using my social security money. I found some mates who helped me kill time during the day but I soon discovered that they were on drugs and booze. They were bad news. One evening I saw some people going into a building. Outside it said something about a Buddhist Society. Some of them seemed about my own age, they weren't all oldies like my Mum and Dad, so I went in and sat at the back. A woman was talking about loving kindness and how we could take hold of our own lives, whoever we were. It made sense. Perhaps I needn't lose my self respect because I hadn't got a job. They met once a week, so I went along on the next Tuesday. This time a couple of lads my own age came and spoke to me. They'd seen me last week. They took me for a coffee. They couldn't find me a job but they gave me friendship and helped me to hang in. The Buddhist message made sense to me and when I did get work a couple of months later everything seemed to hang together. I've got a Buddhist girlfriend too and my parents say they scarcely recognise me for the lad who left home a few years ago.'

A woman who converted to Islam recalls:

'I was fed up with the teasing at work and the jokes. It was almost sexual harassment. Lunch time we were all expected to go to the pub and Friday afternoon was a regular booze-up. This wasn't the life for me. Fortunately I had some Muslim friends who told me about how liberated they felt dressed in modest Muslim clothing, Hijab, and being respected by the men in their society. One of them gave me an English version of the **Qur'an,** the Muslim holy book. It covers almost every aspect of a Muslim's life. I felt that I needed discipline and the Qur'an gave it to me. I needed friends with the same kinds of values as I was looking for. These Muslim women made me feel part of a second family.

Of course, everything hasn't been easy. At work, when I turned up wearing Hijab some of the men laughed. "She's become a Paki!" they said. And pubs were out because Muslims don't drink alcohol. Eventually, I coped with the work issue by deciding to set up my own business. I guess I was lucky. Not everyone might have had the ability to do so. At home, my parents were understanding. My new name, Aishah (she was wife of the Prophet **Muhammad,** and is sometimes called the Mother of Believers), caused no problem. My mum liked it very much. But Muslims don't eat pork and will only eat meat killed in a special way. So no more bacon and eggs! The easiest solution was to become a vegetarian at home, so that is what I am. For a delicious meat meal I go to my friends, who are also teaching me Arabic.'

Girls at a Muslim school in Bradford wearing Hijab. It has become increasingly popular in recent years

Conversions in the future

The earliest religions were tribal or national, like that of the ancient Egyptians, for example. Then came the great religions such as Buddhism, Christianity and Islam, which tried to persuade people about the truth of their message. However, their influence was usually in certain countries, such as the British colonies of the 19th century or the medieval Arab empires. Now Britain, for example, has over a million Muslims, about half a million Sikhs, almost as many Hindus, about 300,000 Jews, many Buddhists and people of many other faiths. Contact with faiths other than our own, if we have one, will grow. Conversions may increase, though often meeting with men and women of other traditions results in one's own beliefs being strengthened, as believers think them out more carefully.

Tasks

1. What made the people in the examples you have read about above decide to change their religions?

2. Discuss some other reasons which might encourage someone to change from one religion to another.

3. What kinds of things might deter someone from changing?

4. How might a mixed marriage between a Hindu and a Jew, for example, be made to work?

11

5 | Spiritual feelings – the human spirit

'My spirit reached out and became one with the spirit of the sea and sky'

This experience had a profound effect on me. It came to me often when I was alone with Nature. It swept over me as I looked out to the stars at night. It was a continuous inspiration. I felt that I was more than an individual. The life of all time was within me and about me. I must serve it.'

At one with all that is

Dr James Hemming, humanist, writer and psychologist, described the spiritual experience like this:

'The human brain has been described as the most wonderful three and a half pounds of living matter in the entire universe. It enables us to think, feel, imagine, speak, and to relate to everything around us. We can learn and remember, plan ahead, feel happy and sad, enjoy the company of others.

But, more than that, our senses can leap into supreme heights of wonder, appreciation and ecstasy as we look at beautiful things, listen to lovely music or, in other ways, reach out beyond our everyday selves. This is the realm of spiritual experience. By sharing in this ultimate awareness, we feel at one with all that is and seek to measure up to the best within us.'

At one with all life

Lord Fenner Brockway, a **humanist**, spent his long life working in Parliament and abroad for the causes of peace, social justice and international understanding. This commitment grew from an experience he had as a young man, watching a sunset over the Irish Sea:

'This spiritual experience came one evening as I stood looking over the green ocean towards the red sunset. A great calm came over me. I became lost in the beauty of the scene. My spirit reached out and became one with the spirit of the sea and sky. I was at one with the universe beyond. I seemed to become one with all life. ►

Inside or outside?

Lord Brockway thought that his overwhelming feelings came from inside himself. He wrote:

'I have said that this experience is my religion, yet it leaves me an agnostic. I suppose some might describe it as communion with God, yet I have no sense of a personal God. My philosophy is founded on the experience I described. I cannot be other than a world citizen, identifying with all peoples.'

Human spirit and holy spirit

The difference in view that Fenner Brockway describes is one that has existed since human records began. In ancient Greece, 2,500 years ago, some thinkers believed that all our experiences are based in the natural world in which we live. Others, however, believed that there is another dimension of reality. This is why many religious people believe that 'spiritual' is about experiences when God reaches them with what they would describe as the holy spirit.

Humanists, however, believe that experiences of the kind that Lord Brockway describes arise from our human consciousness.

Tasks

1   Fenner Brockway described the intensity of his feelings when he watched a beautiful sunset. Have you had a similar experience? Perhaps it was the view from a mountain peak, or seeing a new-born baby, or after some demanding physical achievement (such as a long cross-country walk for your Duke of Edinburgh Award), or listening to a particular piece of music.

2   Think about your memories of these intense feelings. Do you think that these 'peak experiences' came from inside you? Or is it your belief that they came from some outside source? Do you think it is possible that both were involved?

3   Make a start on an anthology that will reflect your own opinions on the human spirit. Look for poems, extracts from prose and plays, pictures and news items to put in it. You might like to start by looking through this book for ideas that ring a bell with you. In the Humanism section you will find pages that talk about our feelings of wonder and mystery – at the cycle of birth and death; at the origin and immensity of the Universe; at the billions of years of the evolution of life on Earth; at the potential of the human spirit to face challenges, and also about our awareness of the need to protect our environment, and our sense of being part of all life on the planet.

Amazonian Indians amongst the ruins of the rainforest, their home (see Task 3)

The human story

A 400-year-old journey

You probably know how to find your way at night. If you look at the stars and find the Pole Star (Polaris), you know that you are facing north.

But the light you see twinkling from Polaris left that star nearly 400 years ago! Since the time when Queen Elizabeth I was on the throne, it has been travelling at nearly 6 million miles pe year until it reached your eye.

The Pole Star and the Sun are both in our galaxy, the Milky Way, which contains a hundred thousand million stars. The Milky Way is itself one of many galaxies. We live in a very big Cosmos.

Our early human ancestors

The spirit of investigation

Seneca, a thinker in Roman times said:

> 'A single lifetime would not be enough to investigate a subject as vast as the sky ... Our universe has something for every generation to investigate ... Nature does not reveal her mysteries once and for all.'

T H Huxley (the man who first used the word 'agnostic' – 'not knowing') wrote in 1887:

> 'We stand on an island in the midst of an ocean of inexplicability. Our business in every generation is to reclaim a little more land.'

Albert Einstein, a very famous scientist, wrote in 1934:

> 'The fairest thing we can experience is the mysterious. It is the fundamental emotion that stands at the cradle of true art and true science. He who does not know it and can no longer wonder, no longer feel amazement, is as good as dead, a snuffed-out candle.'

Our planet emerges

As the vast, hot clouds of gas of the universe cooled, planets, stars, suns and galaxies were formed. The Earth emerged about four and a half billion years ago. For millions of years it was lifeless. Then, as it cooled, single cell

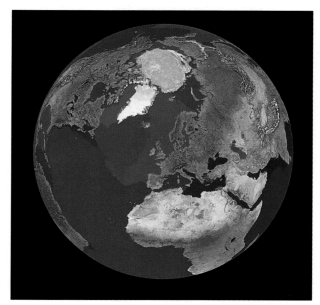

The Earth from space

David Attenborough: 'Such vast periods of time baffle the imagination'

Living things have adapted to the varying climates and environments. Millions of species have flourished and then become extinct – such as the dinosaurs. Our first human ancestors appeared about three and a half million years ago.

In *Life on Earth*, the book of David Attenborough's TV series, he writes: 'Such vast periods of time baffle the imagination.' As life on Earth started three and a half billion years ago, he asks us to compare this to the 365 days in one year – in which one day equals 10,000,000 years. On this time scale, the earliest human beings appeared at 10.30 pm on 31 December!

organisms evolved from chemical interactions within the warm pools and seas of the early world. These first simple cells slowly became built up into the more elaborate cells of which all living creatures are composed. These were the early stages of the long process of evolution.

The restless Earth

The Earth is always changing. The ocean bed has been thrust up into high mountain ranges – the top of Mount Everest was once under the sea. The climate has often changed and great areas were covered with ice or with tropical forests.

Tasks

1   Einstein wrote:

> 'I cannot conceive of a God who rewards and punishes his creatures or who has a will of the type of which we are conscious in ourselves. An individual who should survive his physical death is beyond my comprehension.'

What do you think about the concept of an all-powerful creator God?

2   Imagine it is midnight and you are looking up at countless stars. Write a poem or prose piece on your response to what you see.

3   We modern human beings carry within us abilities from our long evolutionary past (for instance, the skills that were needed for success in growing crops and rearing children). Make a list of some of these. Does understanding these drives help us on our 'inner journey' to understand ourselves?

7 A new life begins

Mother and baby

The child

'A child is the focus of a feeling of love and gentleness from everyone. People's souls soften and sweeten when one speaks of children. The whole of humanity shares in the deep emotions which they awaken. The child is a well-spring of love.'

These words by Maria Montessori (a famous teacher and educationalist) express the intensity of our feelings when a baby arrives. Many people say that it is the most important experience in their lives and one that affects them very deeply.

Our child

'Now this is the day,
Our child,
Into the daylight ►

► You will go out standing,
Preparing for your day.

Our child, it is your day,
This day.
May your road be fulfilled.
In your thoughts may we live,
May we be the ones whom your thoughts will embrace.
May you help us all to finish our roads.'

A Zuni Indian poem

The firstborn

'What have I got exactly? And what am I going to do with her? And what for that matter will she do with me?

I have got a daughter, whose life is already separate from mine, whose will already follows its own directions ... ►

> ► She is the child of herself and will be what she is. I am merely the keeper of her temporary helplessness ... I want her to be free from fear to enquire and get answers, free to imagine and tell tall tales, free to be curious and to show enthusiasm, and free at times to invade my silences.'
>
> From *The Firstborn* by Laurie Lee

How humanists welcome a baby

Humanists share this sense of wonder and love for babies. The arrival of a baby is a time for reflection, as well as joy. In this reflection is an awareness that countless other human beings throughout the millions of years of humanity's evolution have felt the same joy.

Humanists do not hold a religious service to mark a baby's arrival because they see it as part of the natural process of life. They do not see it as a gift from god or gods.

The purpose of a Humanist ceremony is to welcome and name the baby and for the parents to express their commitment to the child's future.

Humanist naming ceremonies

Each Humanist Naming Ceremony is different, as the parents choose their own formats. This excerpt conveys some idea of the kind of wording used:

Officiant: Judith and Graham, you have brought Nicholas here today to be welcomed by your families and friends and to give him his own individual name. As Humanists, we do not commit our children to any one set of beliefs: we commit ourselves to helping them find truth for themselves.

Will you do all you can to provide a loving and stable home for Nicholas, and to help him become a responsible, self-reliant, caring person, and will you love and cherish his uniqueness and help him to develop in his own way?

Parents: We will.

The new arrival

Tasks

1   How soon after birth have you seen a baby? Was it in your family, or at friends' or neighbours' homes? Describe the occasion – what you noticed about the baby, the reactions of the parents and others. What were your feelings about it? Many people are surprised by how deeply they feel – were you? Did it affect the way you look at life in any way?

2   What would you wish for a new life entering this world? Laurie Lee wanted his little girl to be 'a free spirit', growing up with freedom 'to be curious and to show enthusiasm'. Do you think this is important for a child?

3   The wording of the Humanist ceremony shows that the parents think not only about the child's physical welfare but also about its spirit of individuality. What should the relationship be between parents and their children as they grow up to be adults? Should there be some rules? How should these be decided?

The last goodbye

Ideas about death

> 'When we shall be no more, nothing will have power to stir our senses.'
>
> From *On the Nature of the Universe*
> by Lucretius (96–55 BCE)

The word agnostic means 'not knowing'. Humanists think that nobody can know for certain what happens after death. They are not convinced that there is evidence to show that there is life after death. They think that we human beings reach the end of life just like all other living creatures.

The Humanist tradition started in Ancient Greece. Epicurus, a philosopher, chose for his epitaph the words: 'I was not. I have been. I am not. I do not mind.'

These words can still be seen, inscribed on the graves of the followers of Epicurus in countries around the Mediterranean Sea.

A Humanist funeral

Epicurus

How humanists say a last farewell

As humanists do not accept the idea of a god, or heaven or hell, there are no prayers or hymns at a Humanist funeral. The ceremony is a time to reflect on the cycle of birth and death, which is the pattern of all life on Earth. Humanists also make the occasion a celebration of the life that has ended and honour the essential personality, or spirit, of that person.

We all need to grieve when a loved one dies. Humanists feel that a ceremony of this kind helps mourners to accept their grief in a positive way. It also gives a focus for the memories in which the dead person will live on in the minds of those who remain.

The ceremony always includes a quiet time for reflection and for silent prayer by religious people who may be present. Some humanists donate their bodies to medical research. Most are cremated and some ask for ashes to be scattered at a favourite place. These lines (from

Lucretius, explaining the views of Epicurus) are then very suitable:

> 'The seeds that once we were take flight and fly,
> Winnowed to earth, or whirled along the sky,
> Not lost but disunited. Life lives on.
> It is the lives, the lives, the lives that die.'

Life is like a river flowing to the sea

Bertrand Russell was a famous figure of the 20th century. He was a writer, a philosopher and a mathematician. He also devoted his life to working for peace and went to prison for his objections to the terrible slaughter of World War I. Here are his views on life and death:

> 'An individual human existence should be like a river – small at first, narrowly contained within its banks, and rushing passionately past boulders and over waterfalls. ▶

> ▶ Gradually the river grows wider, the banks recede, the waters flow more quietly and – in the end – without any visible break, they become merged in the sea, and painlessly lose their individual being.
>
> The man or woman who, in old age, can see his or her life in this way, will not suffer from the fear of death, since the things they care for will continue.'

Tasks

1 Bertrand Russell was a humanist. What do you think about his views on life and death – and that after death we 'painlessly lose our individual being'?

2 How does this differ from the views that religious believers hold?

3 Funerals are occasions when we experience deep feelings and thoughts. Have you been to a funeral? Describe the occasion (unless this would upset you). Did it make you reflect? Did it affect your inner feelings about life?

4 Try writing a poem on the subject. It could be about someone in your family who died, or about a pet or other animal. Could you bring into it your own inner thoughts and ideas on the cycle of life?

5 How can a funeral best help us in our grieving for the person who has died? Should all funeral ceremonies be religious?

6 Do you think that there is some form of life after death? What about animals? Do they have an after-life?

Bertrand Russell

9 | We need each other

No man is an island

John Donne was a remarkable poet who lived in Shakespeare's time. He wrote some words that are often quoted:

> 'No man is an island entire of itself …
>
> Any man's death diminishes me because I am involved in mankind.'

The happy human

Look at the Humanist symbol below. It represents the Humanist view that, as we only have one life to live, we should try to make it happy and satisfying for every human being.

'Remember your humanity – and forget the rest'

These words were said by Bertrand Russell, a leading humanist. He believed that the human spirit found happiness in thinking of others, by remembering our shared humanity. Some examples are the humanists who played an important part in the work of the agencies set up by the United Nations to try to improve conditions throughout the world.

The Humanist symbol

The UN General Assembly

Since 1945 the countries of the world have sat down together to try to work for a happier and more peaceful world. They do this through the UN Security Council and the UN Agencies. They include:

FAO (Food & Agriculture Organization)'– which works to stop world hunger and relieve famine. Its first Director was a humanist, Lord Boyd-Orr.

UNESCO (UN Educational, Scientific & Cultural Organization) – which has been specially concerned with ending illiteracy, knowing that people who cannot read and write find it hard to improve their standard of living. Sir Julian Huxley, a humanist, founded UNESCO.

WHO (World Health Organization) – its work to prevent illness and malnutrition was directed by Dr Brock Chisholm, a Canadian humanist.

Standing in other people's shoes

Many school students have enjoyed Harper Lee's book (and the film) *To Kill a Mockingbird*. If this includes you, you may remember the time when Scout, the five-year-old daughter of Atticus, comes home from school after an upset with her teacher. Her father says to her:

'If you can learn a simple trick, Scout, you'll get along better with all kinds of folks. You never really understand a person until you consider things from his point of view – until you climb into his skin and walk around in it.'

In J B Priestley's play *An Inspector Calls,* the Inspector tells the Birling family that their greed and selfishness have caused the tragic death of a young woman and says: 'We don't live alone. We are members of one body. We are responsible for each other.'

These writers not only told excellent stories; they wanted also to make us think about the human behaviour that is shown in them. Have you been helped on your 'inner journey' to understand yourself, and other people, by a novel, play, film, TV programme, poem or song?

The Golden Rule

About 2,500 years ago the great Chinese thinker, Confucius, said: 'Do not do to others what you would not like for yourself.'

In other words, imagine yourself in somebody else's shoes! This thought has been echoed many times since then and can be found in many of the world's religions and ethical traditions.

Tasks

1   Many young people get great satisfaction from helping other people. Has this been your experience? Was it, for instance, looking after younger children in your family, or at a nursery? Working with disabled children? Doing something for elderly people, neighbours, relatives or residents at a rest home?

Write something about it, either as an account in diary form – how you felt at first (possibly very nervous!), what you had to do, how you feel about it now; or as a poem that brings out your feelings.

2   Share experiences with your group. Think about this spirit that moves us to give up our own time to help others. Does it come from inside ourselves? Or is it an impulse that comes to us from outside?

3   Talk about times when you wished that other people would remember The Golden Rule of Confucius. And, perhaps, times when you forgot it.

4   Talk about selfishness – what causes it? Are selfish people really happy? What is missing from their inner life? Can selfish people be 'spiritual,' using that word in its widest sense?

Mother and child in UNICEF immunization campaign, Nigeria

What a wonderful world!

The natural world

'The force that through the
green fuse drives the flower
Drives my green age ...
... that drives the water through the rocks
Drives my red blood ...'

These words from a poem by Dylan Thomas bring out the deep feelings that many people experience. They feel a closeness to the natural world and they feel that we draw on the same energy that makes plants grow and the clouds move.

Lord Brockway, a humanist, wrote vividly about his response to watching a beautiful sunset over the Irish Sea:

'Gradually my spirit reached out with what seemed the spirit of the sea and sky. I was at one with the universe beyond. I seemed to become one with all life.'

(You can read more of what Lord Fenner Brockway said on pages 12–13.)

'I see trees so green'

Time to stand and stare

'I see trees so green, red roses too,
Clouds so white, skies so blue,
And I think to myself:
"What a wonderful world!"'

Perhaps you have heard Louis Armstrong, the famous jazz musician, sing this, one of many songs and poems that inspire us to turn away from the routine of everyday life and reflect on the beauty and wonder of the world we live in.

But how many people take time to reflect on this 'wonderful world'? This is the theme of a poem by W H Davies:

Fenner Brockway

'What is this life if, full of care,
We have no time to stand and stare?
No time to stand beneath the boughs
And stare as long as sheep or cows?

No time to see, in broad daylight,
Streams full of stars like skies at night?...

A poor life this if, full of care,
We have no time to stand and stare.'

How ordinary is 'ordinary'?

Norman MacCaig is another poet who thinks we should take time to look at the natural world and reflect on how much we take it for granted.

An ordinary day

'I took my mind a walk
Or my mind took me a walk –
Whichever was the truth of it.

The light glittered on the water
Or the water glittered in the light.
Cormorants stood on a tidal rock

With their wings spread out,
Stopping no traffic. Various ducks
Shilly-shallied here and there

On the shilly-shallying water.
An occasional gull yelped. Small flowers
Were doing their level best

To bring to their kerb bees like
Aerial charabancs. Long weeds in the clear
Water did Eastern dances, unregarded

By shoals of darning needles. A cow
Started a moo but thought
Better of it ... And my feet took me home

And my mind observed to me,
Or I to it, how ordinary
Extraordinary things are or

How extraordinary ordinary
Things are, like the nature of the mind
And the process of observing.'

The environment

'Leave them a flower, some grass and
a hedgerow,
A hill and a valley, a view to the sea,
These things are not yours to destroy as
you want to,
They're a gift given once for eternity.'

These words from Wally Whyton's song, *Leave Them a Flower,* sum up the concerns of many people today that we are destroying our environment, the gift to us from our evolutionary past, without thought for future generations.

Humanists share this concern. Because they believe that human beings have evolved as part of the natural world, they have a deep sense of responsibility towards safeguarding and preserving it. An example of this is Sir Julian Huxley, a humanist, who helped to found the World Wildlife Fund (now the Worldwide Fund for Nature).

Tasks

1   Do you agree with these poets – that today we do not have enough time to look at the world around us and to reflect on what we see?

2   Do you regard yourself as being religious? Or do you hold a humanistic viewpoint, or some other outlook? If so, does your belief help you to look, both outward and inward as these poets do, and to reflect on such experiences? List the main concerns that members of your group have about the environment. (Think about other parts of the world as well as our own.)

3   Make a group anthology of poems, songs, prose excerpts, press items that might make people stop and reflect about these matters.

Facing challenges

Overcoming Everest

Mount Everest is five and a half miles high – the highest point of the Earth's surface. George Mallory was asked his reason for wanting to climb it. He replied: 'Because it's there.' Sadly, he died in 1924, when near the summit.

In 1953 the mountain was at last climbed and Hillary and Tenzing stood on the summit. The leader of this successful team, Sir John Hunt, said of their success:

> 'It seems to symbolize humanity's struggle to come to terms with the forces of nature. The justification for climbing Everest will lie in the seeking by others of their 'Everests', who will be stimulated by this event as others were before us.'

The human spirit overcomes many other 'Everests' or difficult challenges.

Highest on Earth – Mount Everest

Challenging racial injustice

Nelson Mandela was sent to prison for fighting against the injustice of the apartheid system in South Africa. He was subjected to very harsh conditions but his spirit was never broken. He never gave up hope or his struggle for a democratic South Africa.

After 26 years of imprisonment, he was released. When the first free elections were held, he became President of his country.

Nelson Mandela at the United Nations in 1990

Challenging cancer

The Marie Curie Foundation does valuable work to fight cancer. Many lives today are saved by radiotherapy, based on the use of radium. This substance was discovered by the courage of a remarkable wife and husband team. We now are aware of the dangers of radiation sickness but it was not understood when Marie and Pierre Curie started their pioneering work. Their health was badly affected but their humanistic views sustained their spirit of determination to challenge the scourge of cancer. They were awarded Nobel Prizes for their work.

Marie and Pierre Curie at work on radium

Tasks

1 Give some examples of people whose human spirit has helped them to face great challenges. You could write about individuals. (Here are a few names to get you started: Helen Keller, Christy Brown, David Blunkett.)

Or you could write about groups of people – for instance, those who take part in sporting events for the disabled, or the Suffragettes, who challenged the law that only men were allowed to vote.

2 In your group, share your experiences on facing, and surmounting, challenges.

Was it:

- swimming your first 50 metres?
- appearing on a stage, or giving a talk?
- dealing with a sad occasion in your family?
- overcoming a problem with your school studies?

or something else?

3 Reflect on the experiences you discussed and write down your thoughts. What were your feelings at the time? How did you feel afterwards? Did the experience help you to grow as a person? If you found an unexpected strength to overcome a challenge, do you think that it came from your inner resources, or did it seem to be the result of an influence outside yourself?

Overcoming the challenge of disability

First steps

West is changing its exotic image to meet the needs of a new generation of followers.

Satisfied with material comforts?

The Buddha taught that when you search for and find a spiritual path you become an 'inner' person. 'Outer' people are only interested in satisfying material needs; 'Inner' people feel that there is more to life.

Some people find that what they are searching for is explained in Buddhist teachings. They find that spiritual understanding helps them to satisfy their inner needs and improve the quality of their lives.

Engaging on a Buddhist path

Buddhists do not generally think that theirs is the only spiritual path. They believe that people should decide for themselves which religion, if any, is right for them.

There are many different groups which have developed their own styles of Buddhism. These groups all follow the teachings of the Buddha, but with different emphasis on different practices.

As more and more people recognize the limitations of materialism, they are choosing to become Buddhists, regardless of nationality. Once an Eastern religion, Buddhism in the

Buddhist refuge

There is a difference between people who are interested in Buddhism and those who actually want to become 'Buddhist'. Taking that step is like the difference between going out with someone and entering upon a stable relationship or getting married. That step is called taking refuge. For Buddhists, this means that instead of searching for shelter and security in relationships and worldly possessions, they look for spiritual protection. Taking refuge is like a marriage contract for Buddhists, because they feel that if they make a commitment to the religion, it will make a commitment to them.

The Five Precepts

The Five Precepts are vows taken during the refuge ceremony. They reflect the Buddhist belief that happiness stems from goodness. Goodness is understood to be the quality in people which does not want to harm others and wants everyone to be happy.

The Five Precepts are:

1 to try not to take life

2 to try not to steal

3 to try not to cause suffering through sexual misconduct

4 to try not to lie

5 to avoid taking intoxicants or substances which cloud, confuse or trick the mind.

Some teachers are very realistic and do not impose the last vow on 'new' Buddhists.

The Three Jewels

The Three Jewels form the spiritual roof over Buddhists' heads. They are:

1 the Buddha, or Enlightened One, who taught others about the nature of existence and how to be liberated from it

These two people have just taken the Five Precepts in a refuge ceremony given by a Tibetan Lama. They are wearing the traditional white khatags (scarves) which symbolize the teacher's blessing on the disciples' spiritual paths

2 the Dharma, or Truth: the Buddha's teachings, which help remove ignorance and fear and lead one to enlightenment

3 the Sangha, or Buddhist community: experienced and committed Buddhists who offer help and guidance to others.

Promising to take refuge in The Three Jewels in the morning and in the evening helps Buddhists recall the shortcomings of worldly pursuits. They take a little time each day to remind themselves that their beliefs and commitments will lead them to real peace and happiness.

A refuge prayer

'I go for refuge until I am enlightened,
To the Buddha, Dharma and Sangha.
Through the virtues I collect by giving and
other perfections,

May I become a Buddha for the benefit of all.'

Here's how one Buddhist described how she came to take refuge:

'My life was full, yet I couldn't help this feeling of "So what?" A friend told me about a place where you could get Buddhist teachings. For some reason, I found myself interested. These teachings were extraordinary, yet obvious. Why had I never heard these things before? Was I eating from the forbidden tree of knowledge? I felt that at last I was where I had always wanted to be. I had come home. It wasn't the place or environment. It was like a door opening inside myself and I liked what I saw. I knew who I was. It was like a reunion with something precious I could not remember losing, yet now found, could not imagine ever living without. By the end of that visit I had taken refuge.'

Tasks

1 Think of the times when you need help, advice or comfort. Discuss with a friend what you do when you need 'refuge' and compare your own form of refuge with that of Buddhists.

2 Why do you think some Buddhist teachers might not impose the last vow of the Five Precepts on 'new' Buddhists?

3 Make a list of all the things which bring fear to people. Try to say what it is that makes people scared. From what you know about The Three Jewels, say how you think they might offer protection to Buddhists and help them overcome their fears.

4 Explain what you think Buddhists mean by an 'Outer' person and an 'Inner' person. Give some examples of their different kinds of interests and concerns.

The teachings

A statue of the Buddha in the teaching position on a shrine with offerings set before it

'Practise well the Dharma,
Try not to practise evil:
Who practises the Dharma rests in bliss
Both in this world and the next.'

The Buddha

When the Buddha became enlightened he made a vow that he would stay in the world to teach others how to escape from the cycle of life and death and also become buddhas. He spent the rest of his life teaching others how to become enlightened. Because people differ so much in mental ability, he tailored what he taught so that as many people as possible would understand him.

The Buddha gave 84,000 different teachings between his enlightenment at the age of 35 and his death at the age of 80. At that time, none of his words were written down, so listening was vital. Now, there are many books

on what the Buddha taught, but the importance of hearing the teachings has remained. Buddhists believe that reading does not replace the impact of going to see and listen to a teacher.

Going to see and hear a well-respected and inspiring teacher plays an important part in Buddhists' lives. Good teachers make the teachings beneficial for all types of people in every kind of situation.

This is what one Buddhist Lama (teacher) said about putting the teachings into practice:

'With mental strength even someone with AIDS will live longer. If the mind is happy then the body even looks healthier. One disciple was weak with AIDS but although he was unable to meditate, his positive mind helped him live longer. When a bell makes a sound the potential to make the sound comes from inside the bell. All the problems we have in life come from inside ourselves. It is certain that we are born and will die but it is not necessary always to have to go through this process. We have the energy to change the mind. Death is not arising from a person. The person is arising from death.'

Understanding the scriptures

Buddhists believe that understanding the scriptures means using them to alter our speech and actions and the way we look at things. It's easy to agree with an idea. Most of us agree that war should be avoided, yet every day we are engaged in little wars of our own. One has to come back to an idea again and again, like a dog worrying a bone, until it starts to make an impression on the mind.

It is not easy to change the habits of a lifetime – from what is old and comfortable and comes naturally to new and untried attitudes. Although Buddhists say that the results are immediate and feel good, the effort involved requires determination and a great deal of patience with one's own mind. If we want to help make the world a more peaceful place, Buddhism says that we should start by being more patient with our friends.

Stories and parables

Many Buddhist teachers use stories and parables to get across their meaning, as there is nothing like a story, especially a humorous one, to illustrate a point and drive a message home. Buddha used stories, too – such as this one, about one of his own previous lives as a king:

'Once there was a king. He was given an elephant which was very wild and powerful, so he appointed a trainer to tame it. Finally, he managed to control it. One day the trainer and the king went for a ride on it through a forest and the elephant smelt a female elephant in the distance. Crazy with desire, it started running very fast towards her. The riders were in danger, like balloons blown by the wind, so the trainer advised the king to hang on to the branch of a tree, which saved their lives. The king accused the trainer of having lied about taming the elephant but the trainer replied: "I trained the physical part of the elephant, but not the mind. That is why he ran off. I can't control my own mind, so how can I control the elephant's?'

Empowerments and initiations

Sometimes Buddhists will get an opportunity to have a special teaching, laced with rituals and prayers, from a highly qualified spiritual teacher. These are called empowerments, or initiations and connect the disciples to a particular buddha. A highly qualified teacher is able to invite the buddha, or **deity**, to help the disciples understand their own ability to become a buddha.

This is what one western Buddhist, Laura, said about the effect of Buddhist teachings on her mind:

'Having been a practising Buddhist for fifteen years now, I have so far learned that Buddhism is not about being calm and peaceful all the time. Am I any happier? Sometimes I have to remind myself of what I was like to see what I have become. I think the main differences I experience now are to do with the teachings on impermanence. Everything is always changing, and that includes me. We say we know that, but to live that truth changes the way we relate to problems. Whatever happens, we know they will not last and we start to make a separation between what happens to us and our state of mind. This definitely helps the mind to become less agitated.'

Tasks

1 Can you calm your mind? Try this short meditation: sit in a relaxed but alert position. Close your eyes and concentrate on the feeling at the tip of your nostrils as you breathe in and out. Notice that the air is cool going in and warm going out. Notice what is going on in your mind and try to place your thoughts into thought bubbles which you then send out of the top of your head and 'pop'. Bring your attention back to your breathing. As soon as you notice another thought, let go of it as before, always returning your attention to the simple process of breathing in and out. In this way try to calm and control the thoughts which arise in your mind.

2 When you are in the middle of a problem it seems enormous. Discuss how you think the belief that nothing lasts (what Buddhists call impermanence) might or might not help people cope with problems.

3 Why do you think the Buddha had to make a vow to stay and teach others? Discuss the difference between making promises or vows and just saying you will do something.

14 Prayer

The power of prayer

Most people feel the need to pray at some time in their lives, even if they don't particularly believe in anything. Buddhists believe that prayer does two things:

1 It creates a link between a buddha and an ordinary being, like a 'psychic telephone'.

2 It helps the mind find its own natural strength and wisdom, or what Buddhists call its 'Buddha nature'.

Here is a story which illustrates the power of prayer:

There was once a great meditator, who used to sit by his open window saying his prayers. A pigeon came to his window-sill every day. In time, the pigeon died, but the following year a baby boy was born nearby. When the boy was old enough, he amazed the local people by saying prayers he had never been taught. The yogi knew them to be the prayers he said and with his powerful mind recognized the boy as the reincarnation of the pigeon. The yogi's prayers had not only helped him but had had a calming effect on the mind of the pigeon, which caused its human rebirth.

The benefits of prayer

By praying regularly Buddhists hope to get spiritual benefits, in the same way that going to work regularly provides material benefits. Praying helps Buddhists develop kindness and sensitivity to others. It also helps them make decisions and deal with problems. They believe that prayer keeps them in contact with buddhas.

Not all prayers seem to be answered, and this can provide a test of faith, as in the following story:

Asanga sat in a remote cave, praying for a sign from the Buddha Maitreya. After three years he gave up and headed for town. On the way he saw an old man brushing a stone with a feather. The man said that he was trying to remove the boulder because it was blocking out the sunlight from his house. Asanga took this as a sign that he should keep trying and returned to his cave. But after twelve years he had finally had enough. On his way home, he came across a mangy dog lying in the road, clawing at a wound which was being eaten by maggots. Asanga was so moved he cut off a piece of his own flesh as food for the maggots and offered his tongue to them as transport. He closed his eyes but nothing happened. He opened them to find only Maitreya. Asanga asked: 'Where were you all those years?' Maitreya replied: 'I was there all the time, but your delusions prevented you from seeing me.'

Mantras

Mantra literally means 'tool for thinking'. A mantra is often a brief phrase which holds the essential meaning of a text. It is used to help

A craftsman carving the mantra 'Om mani padme hum' into stones in the Himalayas. These are 'mani' stones

30

the mind become peaceful and to concentrate. Buddhists believe that by repeating mantras their daily lives and spiritual practices will improve.

When asked by a female disciple if reciting a certain mantra could result in enlightenment, the 13th-century Japanese Buddhist master, Nichiren Daishonin, replied:

'Included within the word "Japan" is all that is within the country's 66 provinces: all of the people and animals, the rice paddies and other fields, those of high and low status, the nobles and the commoners, the seven kinds of gems, and all other treasures. Similarly, included within this mantra is an entire teaching consisting of all eight volumes. The spirit within the Buddha's body may appear in just his face, and the spirit within his face may appear in just his eyes ... the mantra is to the teaching as eyes are to the Buddha ... If you ceaselessly recite the mantra then you will be continually reading the teaching ... and the power of this teaching enables anyone to become enlightened.'

Visual aids

Buddhists use shrines as a focus for prayer and meditation. The photo on this page shows a shrine with bowls of water. Each water bowl symbolizes those things in life which humans value, such as food and water, flowers, perfume and music. Buddhists believe that in offering these to the Buddha they are encouraging themselves to be generous and reminding themselves that being a buddha is better than having all the beautiful things in the world you can imagine. Some Buddhists like to put things on their shrine that have personal and individual value, often including photographs of religious teachers.

Here, two Buddhists say how prayer affects them:

'I can't imagine going through a day without praying, now. Before I was ordained I prayed briefly. Now I have many prayer commitments. Some people might ►

A Buddhist in prayer beside a simple shrine

► think that prayer is a waste of time but I find that the more I pray, the more energy I have for other things.'

Steve, a Buddhist monk

'Prayer is powerful. I'm not sure if you actually get in contact with anything outside yourself but you definitely get in touch with something inside yourself. In times of distress I have found that mantras help me cope better. They help to keep me calm.'

Lynne, a lay practitioner

Tasks

1 Buddhists believe that spiritual power is everywhere. Discuss what you think this means.

2 Make a list of the kind of things a Buddhist might pray for. How do they compare with what you might pray for?

3 Make up a phrase or saying which you can use to give you inner strength in times of need. It could be like a magical formula or something that you have read in a poem, which you can use as your own personal 'tool for thinking'.

4 What do you value in life which you would offer if you were Buddhist? Could you offer them literally, like flowers, or would you need to use symbols, e.g. a symbol for your love of nature?

15 | Meditation

Meditation and enlightenment

It was by meditating that the Buddha found the answers to the meaning of life and became enlightened.

> 'The sage collected fresh grass from a grass cutter, and, on reaching the foot of the great tree, sat down and made a vow to win enlightenment. He then crossed his legs, which is the best posture of all because it is so immovable, the limbs being massive like the coils of a sleeping serpent. And he said to himself: "I shall not change this, my position, until I have done what I set out to do!"
>
> For seven days he sat – his body gave him no trouble, his eyes never closed, and he looked into his own mind. He thought: "Here I have found freedom", and he, knew that the longings of his heart had at last come to fulfilment.'
>
> Adapted from *The Acts of the Buddha* by Ashvaghosha (translated by Edward Conze)

Buddha Shakyamuni and the six perfections of the enlightened mind

What is meditation?

Meditation is when you still your body and mind to try to get in touch with your deepest thoughts and feelings. These are usually hidden when we are active. The term 'watching the mind' is used to describe how we can learn to recognize things about ourselves and learn to have some control over what our minds do. This takes practice, just like any other skill in life, and it often takes time before meditating feels natural.

Buddhism says that disturbing feelings like anger, hatred and jealousy are unhappy states of mind which prevent us from being happy and becoming enlightened. It also says that we can control them and get rid of them altogether if we want to. Becoming a person who has only happy states of mind is the goal of meditators. Buddhists call someone who achieves this 'enlightened', or 'buddha'. While the Buddha is the founder of Buddhism, there are many buddhas in the past, present and future.

Benefits of meditation

Meditation helps people become more aware of others in everyday life, and to live in better harmony. Trying to be good gives one the key to feeling more peaceful and happy and limits the likelihood of getting into unpleasant situations.

When you realize that goodness brings peace and happiness, then talking and acting with kindness and consideration become more natural. Meditation should affect your speech and actions as well as your mind.

How to meditate

The best-known position for meditation is sitting in the lotus position, which keeps the body 'like the coils of a sleeping serpent'. This position has been used for thousands of years by people unused to chairs and used to yoga. Many modern Buddhists sit upright, supported on chairs in a quiet and comfortable place.

There are many different meditations, but to begin with Buddhists try to calm the mind by concentrating on their breathing and letting go of their thoughts. Then they can try to get some feeling of what 'the mind' really is.

'At your heart, imagine your mind as a drop of light which is the colour of the sky and the size of a mustard seed. Imagine that this luminous drop of mind expands as far as it can. Find which is larger, the expanded drop or the sky ... This is the nature and expanse of the mind!'

From *The Fine Arts of Relaxation, Concentration and Meditation, Ancient Skills for Modern Minds* by Joel Levey

When to meditate

The mind is said to be clearer first thing in the morning, before it has had time to think and when it is fresh after sleep. Ideally, this is the best time to meditate. However, in practice, Buddhists meditate when they can find a quiet place and some time of their own to do it in.

Most Buddhists will try to find some times in their lives when they can concentrate on their meditation and they will go into **retreat**. This means retreating from the world and separating themselves from all outside demands of work, family and friends. They will spend anything from a day to many years meditating, praying and studying. Buddhists say that this not only helps them to meditate better, but then to make better choices and decisions about life.

'When you strip away all the layers of ideas, tensions and frustrations ... there can be nothing wrong. This is not a fantasy or an escape. This is true. If you can realize this awareness, the world will reveal itself as a source of unending delight.'

Tarthang Tulku

This is how one Buddhist described her first taste of meditation:

'The first time I tried to meditate, it was like torture. I became aware not of my inner wisdom, but of every itch and ache in my body. In a room full of silent people I became very self-conscious, and even swallowing seemed to make a loud noise. I was panic-stricken at the thought that I might cough. That five minutes passed like an hour and it was a relief to open my eyes and relax. I realize now that at that time all that really bothered me was how I appeared to others.

Meditation has increased my self-confidence and given me a source of peace. I can now meditate for 20 minutes without getting distracted. I am still struggling with a very busy attitude to life which is constantly telling me to do things and not just sit. But now, I am more able to let go of negative states of mind instead of hanging on to them as if they were a permanent part of "me".'

Tasks

1   A **Zen** method of meditation is to ask 'What is this?' when confronted with a situation or object. Imagine you are a small child seeing things for the first time and look at your surroundings as if for the first time. Describe an object to a friend without using its name.

2   Buddhists believe that we can change ourselves into better people. What would you like to change about yourself? Write a list and discuss with a friend which things you think are possible to change and which are not, and if these changes would make you a better person.

3   Buddhists meditate to get in touch with their deepest thoughts and feelings. Is there anything that you do which helps you understand yourself better?

Karma

What is karma?

Karma means action. Buddhists believe that everything we think, speak and do leaves a moral mark on us which can't be rubbed out. Somewhere along the line of our lives that deed will cause an outcome, in the same way that doing a test will give a result. This is also called the law of cause and effect. Only through good actions can we build up a karmic bank balance of good effects. In the same way, all bad actions will add to our karmic debts.

> 'Whatever deeds a person may do, be they delightful, be they bad, they make a heritage for him or her; deeds do not vanish without trace'.
>
> From the *Sanskrit Dharmapada*

The eightfold path to enlightenment, taught by the Buddha, outlines how to do things for the right reasons. It is the Buddhists' moral code, and they believe that whoever follows it will accumulate good karma.

The 'hub' of the Wheel of Life

Meritorious practices

Buddhists try and tip the balance of good karma in their favour with meritorious actions. These include repeating mantras, doing prostrations, walking round holy places, turning prayer wheels and drawing pictures or making statues of the Buddha. In the same way that taking exercise quickly improves one's fitness, Buddhists believe that these spiritual activities will quickly increase their good karma.

Reincarnation and purification

Buddhists believe that when they are suffering it is because they have caused others to suffer in past lives. They view their bad experiences as a way of 'using up' past karma. They try to understand the causes, and determine not to cause any more suffering to others, or make any more bad karma for themselves in the future.

The meritorious actions of making offerings of the universe (using the hands in a symbolic gesture), light and incense

Buddhists believe that bad experiences burn up old karma, and if dealt with wisely they can purify their minds as if they were burning rubbish. This is sometimes referred to as 'turning problems into the path', because they transform a bad experience into something positive by learning from it.

Buddhists try to live this life partly in preparation for the next. A Buddhist saying which reflects this belief is:

> 'If you want to know who and what you were in a past lifetime, look at yourself now. If you want to know what you will be in your next lifetime, look at your present actions.'

The picture opposite is of the 'hub' of the Wheel of Life – the Buddhist cosmos. It shows a snake, a pig and a pigeon (or more often, a cockerel), biting each other's tail-ends. They symbolize hatred, greed and ignorance. Buddhists believe these are the main delusions, or unhappy states of mind, which make us create bad karma and bind us to the 'cycle of existence', or **samsara**.

Interdependence

Nagarjuna was an Indian teacher who wrote a letter to a friend which later became a famous Buddhist teaching. This letter and the story which accompanies it illustrate Buddhist beliefs that our actions are all linked with each other and create our existences and relationships.

> 'Fathers become sons, mothers become wives,
> Those who are enemies become friends,
> Friends may become the opposite and change again,
> Cyclic existence holds not a shred of certainty.
>
> He eats his father's flesh and kicks his mother,
> He cradles the enemy he killed in his lap.
> A wife gnaws her husband's bones,
> Cyclic existence can be such a joke!'

Once a couple lived in their house with their son and his wife. The father was fond of fishing and went fishing every day in the nearby lake to catch food for the family. One day a stranger came to the house and made love to the son's wife. The son killed him. In time, the stranger was reborn as their son. Eventually, the old mother died and was reborn as a dog which became their pet. The old father too, in time, died and he was reborn as a fish in the lake. One day, the son went fishing and caught that fish which the family ate. The dog smelt the fish, stole some and ate its bones.

And so you can now see how the son ate his father's flesh and cradled the child that was his enemy and kicked the dog that was his mother!

Views on karma

Here are some western Buddhist responses to the concept of karma:

> 'Some people think that karma seems a cruel way of justifying a child's fatal illness ... saying it's their fault, but isn't it worse to say that it's just chance? I think karma explains perfectly why things happen the way they do, but this doesn't mean that we should abandon our compassion.'

> 'Karma makes sense out of an otherwise senseless world.'

> 'You have to believe in reincarnation to understand karma, although even in one lifetime you can see the effects of your actions.'

Tasks

1. Write down a list of what Buddhists believe are reasons to be good.

2. How would a Buddhist explain the rebirths of the characters in Nagarjuna's story?

3. Which jobs do you think would be least and most suitable for Buddhists, in trying to create good karma?

Pilgrimage

An inspiration

Many Buddhists try to go on a pilgrimage at least once in their lives. They don't have to do this, and it isn't necessary in order to reach enlightenment, but it can have many benefits. Going to places where the Buddha lived and achieved greatness can be very inspiring. It makes the Buddha, often a remote and mythical figure, into a real person. His achievements become real and the goal of enlightenment possible, not just a dream or a figment of someone's imagination.

Receiving blessings

Following in the Buddha's footsteps, thinking about his thoughts and being where he was can be very powerful. Buddhists believe that the places where the Buddha experienced the milestones of his life are holy. This means that they have special spiritual power. They can affect people differently from the way ordinary places do. Buddhists believe that the Buddha's goodness was so great that these places, where he achieved special goodness, have his blessings.

Many Buddhists will tell you that in these holy places they don't feel so negative. They will say that instead of feeling too lazy to say prayers or meditate, they feel like doing nothing else. This is what is meant by blessings. It is as if the Buddha's presence still remains in the atmosphere and is able to help anyone who wants help on the path to enlightenment.

The holy places

The four most holy places were described by the Buddha himself to his closest disciple and personal attendant:

'There are these four places, Ananda, which the believer should visit with feelings of reverence and awe. Which are the four? The place, Ananda, at which the believer can say, "Here the Buddha was born"

The place, Ananda, at which the believer can say, "Here the Buddha attained the supreme and perfect knowledge" (where he attained enlightenment) The place, Ananda, at which the believer can say, "Here was the kingdom of righteousness set on foot by the Buddha" (where he taught his first teaching) The place, Ananda, at which the believer can say, "Here the Buddha passed finally away in that utter passing away which leaves nothing whatever to remain behind" (where he passed into Paranirvana).'

Adapted from the *Maha-parinibbana-suttanta*, (translated by T W Rhys Davis)

A Tibetan girl praying at the most respected holy site, Bodh Gaya. She may well have walked many miles and spent everything she possesses in order to make the pilgrimage

Accumulating merit

The merit obtained while performing meritorious actions and devotions at a place of pilgrimage are said to be multiplied 100,000 times, due to the blessings, so pilgrims make the most of their opportunities. Devotions include prayer, meditation and making offerings, such as lights and flowers, in front of objects that they respect. Here, some westerners describe their experiences on pilgrimage:

'The atmosphere of these places is indescribable, really. The peace and tranquillity really are there. Also, to be among all these incredibly devoted people is quite moving. Some of these people have spent their life savings just to pay homage to a stupa. They are so happy to have made it, that it can be an inspiration in itself just witnessing their faith.'

'I never really understood what people meant when they said that these places are special. They aren't especially beautiful in a conventional way, but they really do affect you. It's like they have an inner beauty which doesn't hit you straight away, but you get to see it if you take the time. It's very easy to be still and calm and just sort of contented.'

'I'm usually very lazy, but I was getting up at dawn and meditating for hours every day for weeks, when I stayed at Bodh Gaya. That's what they mean by "blessings". I wish I could bottle it!'

'India itself was a pilgrimage to me. I've always thought about it as the most spiritual place on earth. I know it is as dangerous as everywhere else, and it's usual for visitors to get ill there, but it opens your eyes to life beyond possessions. It's normal to be an "Outer" person in the West, only interested in material things. In India it's normal to be an "Inner" person, looking at yourself and what you are doing on this planet. In India, people accept doing nothing except thinking as a normal way of life. Living life in the slow lane means you see more, not less.'

An array of butter lamps, which are wicks floating in butter oil, lit around a stupa, or monument to enlightenment, which act as a focus for devotional activities

Tasks

1 Buddhists believe that our busy minds and fast lifestyles hinder us from becoming enlightened. What difficulties do you think Buddhists face trying to practise their religion in the modern western world?

2 Do you think you have to have a religious belief to feel the atmosphere of a religious place? Discuss your views.

3 Buddhists believe that some places are blessed. In your own words, describe what you think they mean by 'blessed' and if you think it is possible for a place to be special because of what has happened there.

Enlightenment

'Don't be frightened – get enlightened!' This slogan has become a popular saying for Buddhists in the West. It is one of the ways in which modern Buddhists share their feelings about enlightenment. What attracts people to Buddhism may be any number of things, from the idea of reincarnation to the idea of goodness triumphing over evil. But thinking about enlightenment is like looking at the stars at night. Mysterious, awesome, inspiring and a long, long way away.

Letting go of the self

Many practising Buddhists are content with the idea of creating good karma for better future lives, and trying to pacify their minds for their present happiness. They do not expect to get enlightened for endless lifetimes, yet. This is not only humility ('I have a long way to go before I reach perfection') but also fear. Letting go of oneself is one of the greatest obstacles to achieving enlightenment, because when you become a buddha, the 'self' or 'ego' is gone forever.

A buddha is one who has stopped all craving or grasping, and has understood the true nature of existence. This is freedom from all suffering and is called Nirvana. This means 'blowing out, extinction of thirst'. It is also called the Ultimate Reality and the Absolute Truth. Descriptions of Nirvana make it sound very pleasant.

> 'The joy of pleasures in the world,
> And the great joy of heaven,
> Compared with the joy of the
> destruction of craving
> Are not worth a sixteenth part.'
>
> Tibetan Udanavarga

> 'The path of peace he goes, to the
> cool state of bliss.'
>
> Lalita-vistara

The Wheel of Life

However, if there is 'blowing out' then it can also sound as if we are extinguished, and that sounds like dying. Although Nirvana is not death, we do have to give up something in order to achieve it. So what is it exactly that Buddhists believe all beings find so difficult to let go of?

The self

Buddhists believe that the 'self' or 'ego' is what binds us to the never-ending circle of life and death, yet we cling to it passionately. It is the 'I', the 'me', the 'mine', that wants pleasure and happiness and enjoyment, and not any suffering. It is the idea that there is something about us which exists separately from everything else. It is this thought which creates suffering for ourselves through selfishness.

In the picture of the Wheel of Life we can see all the realms of samsara. On the outer rim are symbolic pictures of the causes of our bond to this wheel. The thought of giving up the self-love which creates these causes is very threatening to us.

Outside the Wheel of Life, which is held in the jaws of Death, is the Buddha, who points to the cool and peace of the moon, a symbol for Nirvana. Because Nirvana is indescribable and unimaginable, we are unable to rush into its arms. Just as a fish has no experience to understand the nature of land, neither do we have the language to understand Nirvana.

> 'Because Nirvana is expressed as extinction, there are many who have got the wrong idea that it is negative, and expresses self-extinction. Nirvana is definitely not extinction of self, because there is no self to get rid of. If at all, it is the extinction of the illusion, of the false idea of self.'
>
> Adapted from *What the Buddha Taught* by W Rahula

Tantra

Some Buddhists believe that there is a quicker route to becoming enlightened than gradually evolving into a buddha. These Buddhists practise Tantra. Tantra is the path which transforms the energy of desire into the energy to become enlightened. It involves changing the way we look at the world.

> 'Perfection is not something that is waiting for us somewhere in the future: "If I practise hard now maybe I will become a perfect buddha", or "If I behave well in this life and act like a religious person, maybe some day I will go to heaven". According to *Tantra,* heaven is now!'
>
> *Introduction to Tantra* by Lama Yeshe

Enlightened beings

According to some traditions of Buddhism, there are people who live now who are almost enlightened and people who some say, are enlightened. These are reincarnations of past yogis and yoginis who only keep coming back to help others. They are able to control their minds at the time of death so that they can choose their next rebirth. They have the compassionate wish to reach enlightenment only to benefit others.

Many of these bodhisattras are being reborn in the West now, and Buddhists believe that this is because of the rising interest in Buddhism in western countries.

This is how some Buddhists replied when asked about their paths to enlightenment:

> 'How can I get enlightened yet? I've got too many responsibilities. My children need me.'
>
> If you want enlightenment, then you're just wanting again. It is what they call a superior desire. But it's still desire.'
>
> 'All I hope to achieve in this lifetime is a few realizations and to have created the cause for a good rebirth next time round.'
>
> 'There's a story about this yogi who had renounced so much that he dashed out of his cold cave each morning to meditate in the sunlight. There was a thorn bush in front of his cave which used to tear his skin every time he passed it, but he was in such a hurry to get enlightened that he wouldn't stop to cut it back. He was so appalled by the suffering of samsara that he put enlightenment before everything else. That's what I call renunciation!'

Tasks

1 Find out what the twelve pictures on the outer rim of The Wheel of Life symbolize?

2 Buddhists believe that self-love creates suffering. Discuss this or organize a class debate based on this idea.

3 Buddhists describe Nirvana as a state of bliss and freedom from suffering. Write a description of what you think Nirvana feels like, and whether you think it is possible to attain it.

Christian spirituality

What is Christianity?

Christianity is about Jesus. Christians believe that Jesus rose from death three days after his Crucifixion. Easter Day, the anniversary of the **Resurrection**, is the most important day in the Christian year. To the Christian it is the coming of a spiritual Spring. All the first Christians were Jews. Some Jews, but not all, hoped that a deliverer would be sent by God. They called him the **Messiah.** When non-Jews eventually became followers of Jesus they used a Greek term for Messiah (Anointed One): 'Christ'. This explains why his followers are known as Christians and sometimes use the name Christ rather than Jesus.

Christian spirituality is about experiencing Jesus as realistically as his friends, Mary of Magdala, Simon Peter and the other famous disciples did, almost 2,000 years ago. For Christians, Jesus is real and alive, not just a character in a story. Christians sometimes say:

> 'If Jesus Christ a thousand times were born anew,
> Despair O man until he's born in you.'

The purpose of Christian spirituality

Christian spirituality is about becoming one with Jesus. There are many ways, Christians believe, in which God helps people to achieve this. Of course, it is necessary to have faith, but Jesus taught that this did not mean being massively confident. He told his friends:

> 'If you had faith no bigger than a mustard seed, you could say to this mulberry tree, "Be rooted up and planted in the sea", and it would obey you.'

Luke 17:6

In Matthew's Gospel the words are slightly different, but the meaning is the same:

> 'If you have faith no bigger than a mustard seed, you will say to this mountain, "Move from here to there!" and it will move; nothing will be impossible for you.'

Matthew 17:20

This is where the saying 'Faith can move mountains' comes from. Of course, Jesus was using a metaphor to make his point. Christians don't believe that it would be right, even if it were possible, to try to tap into God's power for such purposes as moving mountains. They use mechanical diggers and other machines like everyone else if they want to build a road or a bridge. However, many claim that they have been able to move such mountains as addiction to drugs or alcohol, a violent temper, facing the death of a loved one, divorce, severe illness, failing to make the grade to get into a sports team or pass examinations, or being unemployed. For most human beings these are the real mountains of life. People face different kinds of mountains at different stages of their lives.

Grace

Christians speak about God's grace, by which they mean God's undeserved love, giving them strength. St Paul, the great Christian missionary who wrote many letters in the New Testament, once said that he had a 'thorn in my flesh'. No one knows what it was, but it was very painful. He wrote:

> 'Three times I begged the Lord to rid me of it, but his answer was: "My grace is all you need, power is most fully seen in weakness"... So, I am content with a life of weakness, insult, hardship, persecution, and distress, all for Christ's sake: for when I am weak, then I am strong.'

2 Corinthians 12:8–10

Grace is not a magic wand. It may help individuals to overcome something, but they may still have to put up with it, as St Paul did.

Mysticism

A mystic is a person who experiences the kind of reality many religious people never reach, though they may hope to do so. Perhaps it is better not to try to explain this more, but to let the following poem speak for itself:

'The mystic was back from the desert.
"Tell us", they said, "what God is like".

But how could he ever tell them
what he had experienced in his heart?
Can God be put into words?

He finally gave them a formula
– so inaccurate, so inadequate –
in the hope that some of them might be tempted
to experience it for themselves.

They seized upon the formula.
They made it into a sacred text.
They imposed it on others as a holy belief.
They went to great pains to spread it in foreign lands.
Some gave their lives for it.

The mystic was sad.
It might have been better if he had said nothing.'

Anthony de Mello, from *Transcendence: Prayer of People of Faith* edited by D Faivre

Some Christians have 'seized upon the formula' and tried to impose their brand of religion upon other people, but most of them believe that Jesus can be experienced in many ways. Some have become mystics, finding him in places apart from other human beings, sometimes in desert caves. Daily prayer, reading the Bible and worshipping with other Christians are some of the other ways.
A number of these are covered in the next few pages, but Christians believe that there are many paths to Jesus. Perhaps it is better to say that in the last 2,000 years they have discovered that Jesus reaches out to them in a variety of ways.

The next paragraph sums up the purpose of Christian spirituality:

'Father of all, we give you thanks and praise, that when we were still far off you met us in your Son and brought us home. Dying and living, he declared your love, gave us grace, and opened the gate of glory. May we who share Christ's body live his risen life; we who drink his cup bring life to others; we whom the Spirit lights give light to the world. Keep us firm in the hope you have set before us, so we and all your children shall be free, and the whole earth live to praise your name; through Christ our Lord. Amen.'

The Alternative Service Book 1980

Portrait of Jesus by an Indian Christian artist. What kind of Jesus does he want to depict?

Tasks

1   What could St Paul have meant by writing: 'When I am weak, then I am strong'?

2   Why did the mystic think it might have been better if he had said nothing?

20 Prayer

What is prayer?

Prayer is the most popular way Christians use to get to know God through Jesus. But what is prayer? Often people talk about 'saying prayers', going through some sort of ritual. Teachers in collective worship in school and ministers in churches normally use the Lord's Prayer, but have been known to give it a miss. Many people don't notice whether it's said or not.

Prayer is based on the belief that God cares and is eager to share in the everyday lives of people. Prayer is a conversation, a sharing. For Christians it is like being with a close friend. With such a person we share our problems and our joys but we also chat over a coffee or a Coke simply because we are friends and it's good to be with each other. Sometimes we share our friendship with many others; sometimes we like to be alone together in our room, on a walk or in a quiet place. Sometimes Christians pray alone; sometimes in groups.

Jesus at prayer

Jesus lived close to his father, God, in prayer. We only know of a few crisis occasions, but his disciples asked him to teach them to pray, and this suggests that they were used to seeing him praying.

The most famous account of Jesus at prayer describes the scene in the Garden of Gethsemane, outside Jerusalem, just before his arrest and execution. He went away from his friends, though apparently they could still see him. The perspiration ran off his forehead like drops of blood. He prayed: 'Abba, Father, all things are possible to you; take this cup from me. Yet not my will but yours' (Mark 14:36). 'Abba' was a word which meant father or Dad in Jesus' language, Aramaic.

Jesus prayed. He asked to be spared the painful death of crucifixion, but also accepted his father's decision. Christians believe that it is right to ask God for some things, but not to pray to win the Lottery, for example!

Some Christian prayers

Jesus' friends once asked him to teach them to pray. The result was what Christians describe as the Lord's Prayer. In a modern English translation, the fuller version reads:

> **'Our Father in heaven, may your name be hallowed; your kingdom come, your will be done, on earth as is in heaven. Give us today our daily bread. Forgive us the wrong we have done, as we have forgiven those who wronged us. And do not put us to the test, but save us from the evil one.'**

> Matthew 6:9–13 (see Luke 11:2–4 for a slightly different version)

The prayer offers obedience, asks for help but not luxury, seeks forgiveness from God but recognizes that Christians must first of all forgive those who have wronged them, and asks for deliverance from the test. Originally this probably referred to the threat of persecution.

Christians can pray at any time. Most choose the early morning and just before going to bed, but ideally the whole of life should be a prayer. Some Christians, especially those belonging to churches with origins in Russia or the Balkans, recite the Jesus Prayer whenever they can: on journeys or while having a meal, for example. One form of it is:

> **'Lord Jesus, son of God, have mercy upon me, a sinner.'**

They believe that this is a way of keeping God in mind and of keeping out bad thoughts.

Here are two prayers. The first is from Celtic Ireland, and is the earliest poem surviving from that country.

A Christian prayer meeting

'I am the wind which breathes upon the sea.
I am the way of the ocean.
I am the murmur of the billows.
I am the vulture upon the rocks.
I am the beam of the sun.
I am the fairest of plants.
I am the wild boar in valour.
I am the salmon in the water.
I am a lake in the plain.
I am a word of knowledge.
I am the point of the lance in battle.
I am the God who created the fire in the head.'

The speaker in this poem is God. This may surprise you: we usually think that prayer is human beings talking to God. The Celtic prayer reminds us that prayer is a two-way activity.

The second prayer is very modern. It comes from a prayer book used in New Zealand, and is also in the form of a poem.

'Lord, it is night.
The night is for stillness.
Let us be still in the presence of God.

It is night after a long day.
What has been done has been done,
What has not been done has not
been done.
Let it be.

The night is dark.
Let our fears of the darkness of the
World and our own lives
Rest in you.

The night is quiet.
Let the quietness of your peace enfold us,
All dear to us,
and those who have no peace.

The night heralds the dawn.
Let us look expectantly to a new day,
New joys, new possibilities.

In your name we pray. Amen.'

Tasks

1 Why do Christians feel that it is a privilege to approach God in prayer?

2 Why are the early morning and before going to bed good times for prayer?

3 Discuss why Christians feel that they must forgive others before they can ask to be forgiven?

4 Why would Christians not pray to win the Lottery or a sports match or a war?

5 Describe the kind of world in which the Celtic person lived.

21 The Bible

Jesus as a role model

Many of us have role models, people we turn to and imitate, perhaps someone in sport, or in the media or a lead singer in a band. Jesus is the role model for Christians. They pray as he taught them, and they read the Bible, which tells them about him, especially the part called the New Testament. They try to follow the example that they find there, and his command to them to love God and their neighbours (that is, the people they live with, work with and meet in all sorts of other ways). Jesus was a Jew and he found these teachings in the books of his Jewish heritage, in Deuteronomy 6:5 and Leviticus 19:18. At the time this was the only scripture which the first Christians, who were all Jews, had. None of the books about Jesus, the New Testament, existed.

Jesus knew his **Torah,** (the first five books of the Bible) well. One day, soon after he was aware that he had a special message to preach, he decided that he needed peace and quiet to think about how to do it. He went into the desert, where he fasted and prayed. Ideas came flooding into his mind. Accounts tell of him being tempted by Satan, or the devil. Many Christians believe that there is such a being. Others think of it as the selfish side of their nature, seeking to gain the upper hand in their decision-making. Everyone seems to face this kind of challenge almost every day.
The Bible says:

> 'At the end of his 40 days Jesus was famished. The devil said to him: "If you are the Son of God, tell this stone to become bread." Jesus answered: "Man is not to live on bread alone." The devil led him to a height and in a flash showed him all the kingdoms of the world. "All this dominion I will give you and the glory that goes with it; for it is put into my hands and I can give it to anyone I choose. You have only to do homage to me and it will be all yours." Jesus answered: "Scripture says, 'You shall do homage to the Lord your God and worship him alone'". The devil took him to Jerusalem and set him on the parapet of the Temple. "If you are the Son of God throw yourself down from here, for scripture says, 'He will put his angels in charge of you' and 'They will support you in their arms for fear you should strike your foot against a stone'." Jesus answered him: "It has been said, 'You shall not put the Lord your God to the test'".'

Luke 4:3–10

Notice that Jesus was tempted to doubt and put to the test the scriptures in which he trusted, as well as his own powers. Christians believe that the Bible can help them to develop their spirituality, often linked with prayer.

Using the Bible in a time of need

A teenager was seriously ill. His parents, Harry and Jean, took it in turns to sit by his bedside throughout the night. They were Christians

A page from the Lindisfarne Gospels, written about 1400 years ago by a Northumbrian monk

and prayed for his recovery as other members of the church did. One of their favourite passages was Psalm 23. Part of it reads:

'The Lord is my shepherd; I lack for nothing.
He makes me lie down in green pastures, he
leads me to water where I may rest;
he revives my spirit; for his name's sake he
guides me in the right paths.
Even were I to walk through a valley of
deepest darkness I should fear
no harm, for you are with me; your staff and
shepherd's crook afford me comfort.'

They found short passages like these and took heart from them. This verse is about Jerusalem, but that didn't matter to them.

'No child there will ever again die in infancy,
no old man fail to live out his span of life. He
who dies at a hundred is just a youth, and if
he doesn't attain a hundred years he is
thought accursed!'

Isaiah 41:20

Or Isaiah 41:10:

'Have no fear, for I am with you; be not
afraid, for I am your God.'

The New Testament contains many accounts of Jesus healing sick people or even bringing dead ones back to life. For example, on one occasion he and his disciples were approaching a town called Nain and met the funeral of the only son of a widow. He told her not to weep, put his hand on the stretcher on which the body was being carried and said: 'Young man, I tell you, get up'. The son sat up and began to speak to his mother (Luke 7:11–17). A man named Jairus had a daughter who was sick. He sent for Jesus but she died before he arrived. Jesus went into the room where she lay, took her by the hand and said: 'Get up, my child'. She stood up immediately (Luke 8:41–56).

Sometimes people ask whether these things really happened. Not Jean and Harry. They read the stories for comfort, and to sustain themselves in their faith. Their teenager recovered and grew to be a strong and fit man.

A portrait by an Indian artist, of a woman disciple washing Jesus' feet

However, it doesn't always work that way. Peter and Alice had a lovely healthy daughter called Kim. She was their only child. She was a sixth-former at the local comprehensive school. She had read one of the lessons in church at the special Christmas service. Less than a month later she died suddenly of leukaemia. Her parents remain believers, but it has been hard for them to keep their faith and to accept the fact that God doesn't always give the answer to prayer that people want.

Tasks

1   We all have decisions to make. In groups, discuss the ways you find helpful when making choices, if you are willing to do so. Which ways would Christians add?

2   You may know another version of Psalm 23. If so, compare it with the one used here. Which one do you prefer? Why?

3   What lessons can Christians learn from the story of the temptation of Jesus?

4   Some Christians fast (go without food), as Jesus did in the desert, during the festival of Lent. How might fasting help their spiritual lives?

Pilgrimage

The Crusades

Journeys to special holy places have been important to Christians for centuries. For 1,700 years visits have been made to Bethlehem, Nazareth, and Jerusalem, in what Christians and Jews call the Holy Land, to make pilgrimages to sites of Jesus' ministry, especially Bethlehem, where he was born, and Jerusalem, where his death and resurrection took place.

In 640 CE Jerusalem was captured by Muslim armies. This did not usually cause problems for Christian pilgrims, who were allowed free access to their holy places. Jerusalem and the land of Palestine, of which it was a part, was a place where Jews, Christians and Muslims lived together. However, after 300 years things began to change and the Pope of the day, Urban II, encouraged rulers of Christian countries in Europe to assemble armies and capture the holy places for Christianity. There were several reasons for these 'Crusades', which began in 1095. One was complaints by pilgrims that the Muslim Turks who occupied the country made life difficult for them. That stirred up demonstrations in Christian Europe. Pilgrimage was a risky business. Sometime Christians in the Balkans and Turkey captured travellers and sold them into slavery.

The first Crusade was successful in its aim. Jerusalem was captured in 1099 and was held by the crusaders until 1187 when a Muslim leader called Saladin retook it. This led to the Third Crusade, made famous to the British because King Richard the Lionheart was one of its leaders. However, it did not succeed. Many crusaders were sincere pilgrims. The motives of others may have been less honourable.

Pilgrimage today

Rome, Lourdes, Knock (in Ireland), and Walsingham (in England) are other well known places for Christian pilgrimage, often because visions of the Virgin Mary have been seen.

Lourdes is associated with the healing of sick people, and many who are ill go in the hope of being cured. One pilgrim described the experience:

> 'I have been to Lourdes once. It was an amazing experience. The concentration and prayer which came from people's suffering and desire for healing was very powerful, I found, and very moving. I also found the commitment to looking after the sick very inspiring, as was the great faith of the people I met. I have been to Jerusalem and to Rome, but was not as impressed at the level of faith as I was at Lourdes.'

Another pilgrim said:

> 'I have been to Lourdes for an Easter visit and would like to go again as part of a group. It was a very intense place of concentrated spirituality and I was very moved by the fact that so many different countries were represented in one place.'

Some travel agents specialize in organizing pilgrimages

Sick people on their way to Lourdes. There is never a lack of volunteers eager to help them

During the Roman occupation of Britain there were many Christians in the country. The most famous was probably St Patrick, who was born about 390 CE. Then new settlers known as Anglo-Saxons began to colonize Britain. They were not Christians and, except in the west of the country, Christianity died out. However, it flourished in Ireland, and monks from that land decided to reconvert Britain. Iona, a Scottish island, and Holy Island or Lindisfarne, off the coast of Northumbria, are places where monasteries were founded by missionaries who brought Christianity to Britain. Pilgrims from many denominations go to them, and they are particularly popular with young Christians. At Iona a community was set up in 1938 by the Reverend George MacLeod, and the ruins of the old monastery were rebuilt. Members of the community live there for a period of time each year, to recharge their spiritual batteries before leaving to work in industrial areas or overseas missions.

Most of the places where pilgrims go could be visited by tourists, but something would be missing. Tourists would look at the architecture and stained glass, and read about the history in their guide books. Pilgrims may not notice the buildings, though they would probably be aware of the history to some extent. What they seek to do is to experience a spiritual presence.

The place has been made holy by the visits and prayers of pious women and men over many centuries. They hope to share in it. New places of pilgrimage keep coming into existence. Someone may have a vision of the Virgin Mary or a Christian may be put to death for being loyal to the faith. That person's grave or site of martyrdom might become a place of pilgrimage and eventually attract many Christians.

Tasks

1   What experiences have you had that compare with the feelings of the pilgrim to Lourdes in the first quote? Explain why they were so amazing.

2   Many pilgrims who went to Lourdes in hope of a cure came home no better physically but they returned satisfied. Why do you think this happened?

3   Invite someone who has been on a Christian pilgrimage to your school. Find out what it meant to them.

4   It may be possible to get members of different faiths together to discuss their experiences as pilgrims. Try to arrange such a meeting.

23 / Worship

This is the most popular or common Christian activity. It happens worldwide every Sunday and often on other days and is made up of singing, reading from the Bible, praying and listening to someone give a sermon (a talk to lift up the heart and give encouragement and inspiration or make people think). At least one group, The Society of Friends, worships in a totally different way, which will be discussed later.

Hymns

The first Christians were Jews and they sang the psalms which they found in their scriptures. Soon they composed their own songs, and have done ever since. These religious songs are called hymns.

Amazing Grace is a hymn which is still very popular, 200 years after it was composed. Its four verses are:

> 'Amazing grace, how sweet the sound
> That saved a wretch like me!
> I once was lost but now am found,
> Was blind but now I see.
>
> Through many dangers, toils and snares
> I have already come;
> God's grace has brought me safe thus far,
> And he will lead me home.
>
> The Lord has promised good to me,
> His word my hope secures;
> He will my shield and portion be
> As long as life endures.
>
> And when this heart and flesh shall fail
> And mortal life shall cease,
> I shall possess within the veil
> A life of joy and peace.'

Amazing Grace was written by John Newton, a man who took black slaves from Africa to North America until he became a Christian. It is one of only a few hymns which have proved equally popular among white and black Christians.

Hymns are still being composed. One of the most famous of recent times is by Sydney Carter, and is known as *The Lord of the Dance*. These are three of its verses and the chorus:

> 'I danced in the morning when the world was begun,
> And I danced to the moon and the stars and the sun,
> And I came down from heaven and I danced on the earth,
> At Bethlehem I had my birth.
>
> (Chorus):
>
> Dance, then, wherever you may be,
> I am the Lord of the Dance, said he,
> And I'll lead you all, wherever you may be,
> I'll lead you all in the dance, said he.
>
> I danced on a Friday when the sky turned black –
> It's hard to dance with he devil on your back.
> They buried my body and they thought I'd gone;
> but I am the dance and I still go on.
>
> They cut me down and I leapt up high;
> I am the life that'll never, never die.
> I'll live in you if you'll live in me:
> I am the Lord of the Dance, said he.'

A woman priest celebrating the Eucharist. Women play increasingly important roles in many Christian groups

A Society of Friends' meeting for worship

Sermons

A sermon is a talk given during a service, often by the person leading it, to explain Jesus' teachings or encourage the congregation in living their everyday lives. These days it lasts about fifteen minutes, but a century ago it was not unusual for someone to preach for an hour. Sometimes an hour-glass was placed near the pulpit and the minister was expected to speak until all the sand had run into the bottom. There is a story that a preacher was tiring and longing for the sand to run out when a man came forward, turned it upside down and expected him to continue for an hour longer!

Dancing and plays

Sometimes dance dramas and plays are performed in churches. They had their place in services long ago, but when they were re-introduced from the 1960s some Christians were upset. They felt that God's house should not be treated like a dance hall!

An exception to the rule

One group does not engage in the kind of worship found among most Christians. They are called The Society of Friends. If you go to their meeting houses (they do not use the word 'church'), you are likely to find them sitting silently in a square or circle, facing one another. They argue that God is not in the pulpit or the altar or the communion table, but within every human being. They believe that in looking towards one another they are looking towards God. They talk about 'that of God in everyone'. They wait upon the holy spirit in silence and only speak if they are convinced that the spirit wants them to. A whole meeting, lasting about an hour, may pass in total silence. On the other hand, many people may feel prompted to speak.

Tasks

1 Hymns are supposed to be uplifting. Why and how would John Newton's hymn encourage slaves? Which verse would they treasure most? Why?

2 What is the message of *The Lord of the Dance?* Listen to a recording of it if possible; if not, think about why the verses are so popular. (Two verses have been omitted because they can be read as being anti-Jewish.)

The Eucharist

The Resurrection

On the day of Jesus' **Resurrection**, two of his disciples, perhaps husband and wife, were making their way to a village, Emmaus, about seven miles from Jerusalem. They were aware of rumours of the Resurrection and were arguing with one another about the events of the past few days. A stranger caught up with them and joined in the discussion. He began to remind them of verses in the Torah which, he said, referred to Jesus. When they reached Emmaus they asked him to stay with them, as nightfall was approaching. They ate supper together. During the meal Jesus, for that is who it was, took bread, made the blessing which Jews speak before eating, broke the bread, and offered it to them. At that moment they recognized him, and he vanished.

What actually happened could be debated for the rest of our lives, as we were not there. Christians have different explanations for this story, but all agree that it was a penny-dropping situation: the moment of recognition was a moment of truth. Although night time was a risky time to travel and the couple must have been tired, they set off back to Jerusalem to share their experience with the rest of the disciples, who, they found, had their own accounts to share with them. Since then Christians have always felt that Jesus is a guest at their table.

What is the Eucharist?

As you walk past a church you might look at the notice board. One of the services which will be listed is the Eucharist or it might be called the Mass, Holy Communion, the Lord's Supper, the Divine Liturgy, or the Breaking of the Bread. What matters is not the name but the meaning. At the Eucharist Christians pray that Jesus may be known to them now, 2,000 years later, in the breaking of bread. This is a symbolic meal which Christians share together.

A group of Christians taking Communion

Four days earlier than the journey to Emmaus, the two travellers may have been present at the last meal which Jesus shared with his disciples. It was a supper. Jesus took bread, broke it, and said: 'This is my body, which is given for you'. Taking the cup of wine from which everyone usually drank, he said: 'This is my blood, which is shed for many'. He commanded them, whenever they shared a meal together to remember him. 'Do this in remembrance of me', he said, and told them that he would be with them when they did. Possibly, at Emmaus, the two disciples were the very first to discover what Jesus actually meant by what he had said and done four days earlier. Day by day, week by week, or in some churches only once a year, Christians share the Last Supper symbolically, and believe that they experience the presence of Jesus in it.

You can read the full road to Emmaus story in the Gospel of Luke, chapter 24:13–35. You can find the Last Supper accounts in Matthew 26: 20–29; Mark 14:17–25 and Luke 22:14–20. If you read all of them, look for the message, rather than arguing about the dissimilarities.

Different forms of service

The way the Communion service is conducted varies as much as the name by which it is called. At one extreme there may be great simplicity. The group of Christians stand in a circle and invite one of them to act as leader. She or he will usually read one of the Last Supper accounts. It might be the first version to have been written down, which is contained in St Paul's first letter to the Christians at Corinth (chapter 11: 23–5). The Gospels were written at least 20 years later. St Paul wrote: 'On the night of his arrest the Lord Jesus took bread, and after giving thanks to God broke it and said: "This is my body, which is for you; do this in memory of me". At this point the leader may take a small loaf of bread which has been lying on a nearby table, and break off a piece to give to the next person, perhaps saying that persons' name; for example: 'Hannah, receive the body of Christ'. That person will, in turn, take the loaf and say the same words, using the next person's Christian name. Finally, the leader will receive the last piece of bread from the person at his or her side.

The same will happen with a single large cup of wine, known as a chalice. The leader will pick it up from the table and say: 'This is the cup of the new covenant sealed by my blood. Whenever you drink it, do this in memory of me'. Then the chalice will be passed from Christian to Christian, just as the bread had been a few moments earlier. Somewhere in the service there will be some prayers. A hymn may be sung. But the essence is the simple receiving of bread and wine and an awareness of the presence of Jesus among them.

Another form of Communion service. This is sometimes called the breaking of the bread

At the other extreme, a High Mass has much ceremony; those conducting the service wear special robes and a choir sings wonderful music. However, it must be remembered that the purpose of the ritual is the same: to remember the Last Supper and receive the spiritual food of Jesus' body and blood.

The Society of Friends never celebrates the Last Supper – or it could be said that it always does. Its members may say that whenever they share a meal they repeat the Emmaus road experience.

High Mass in Roman Catholic Westminster Cathedral: a very elaborate Communion service

Tasks

1   What might be going through the minds of the people in the photographs?

2   Someone said: 'When I can't go to Mass I feel guilty and uncomfortable.' Another said: 'I feel starved when I go more than three or four days without the Eucharist.' What do you think they meant?

3   If possible, invite a clergy person to simulate a communion service for you. (See what name is used for the service from the notice board.) Discuss the spiritual importance of the service with them.

4   Why do you think the Lord's Supper is the most spiritual activity for most Christians?

Other forms of Christian spirituality

There are many different ways in which people who believe in God develop and strengthen their relationship with God. Here are a few of the ways used by Christians.

Meditation

Meditation is important for Buddhists and Hindus (see pages 32–3 and 59). Recently, especially as contact has grown between religions, some Christians have also added meditation to their ways of developing spirituality. Other Christians are less happy with this approach. For some people it is strange and not traditional. In the same way, many of us, even if we are young, are often reluctant to try new foods or listen to unfamiliar music. There is another reason. Some Christians think that meditation requires you to empty the mind. If you do, they believe the forces of evil which are lurking nearby will fill the void. This is a misunderstanding of the nature of meditation.

The rosary

Some Roman Catholics and Eastern (Orthodox) Christians use a rosary to help them concentrate when they pray. The Orthodox rosary is made from strands of black wool closely knotted 100 times and tied together in a cross-shaped tassel. As each knot passes between the fingers the Jesus prayer, 'Jesus, son of God, have mercy upon me', is said. Roman Catholics use a circle of beads in ten sets, with a large bead between each ten. A crucifix lies at the end of four beads outside the circle. The Lord's Prayer, ten Hail Marys and the Gloria are said as the beads go through the fingers, and certain mysteries, events in Jesus' life, are remembered. Someone who uses a Catholic rosary recites the Jesus prayer, and says that it leads into silence and the ability to meditate, which is usually difficult to find except as a member of a group.

A group of meditating Christians

Icons

An **icon** is a picture of Jesus, his mother, or a saint, painted on wood. It is a carefully made devotional image. The artist trains for many years, and prepares to produce an icon by prayer and fasting. A special technique known as egg tempera is used. Eastern Christians prefer icons to statues, which they consider too life-like.

Stations of the Cross

In some churches you will see fourteen paintings or sculptures of Jesus, usually seven on each side wall. These show stages of his journey to crucifixion. Sometimes a fifteenth is

A rosary being used as an aid to prayer and reflection

An artist painting an icon

added, of Jesus being laid in the tomb. Often they are used as a pilgrimage. Christians, usually Roman Catholic, stop in front of each, from first to last, and meditate upon Jesus' sufferings. It is like walking along the Via Dolorosa, which means 'Sadness Road', the route taken by Jesus to his death on the hill of Calvary.

There is a great variety in the Christian spiritual practice. Many Christians use the kinds of aids mentioned here but others, such as The Society of Friends and the Salvation Army, do not celebrate the Eucharist or, in the case of Friends, even sing hymns. Sometimes none of the spiritual activities covered on this page or the ones that have gone before it seem to work. The believer just feels spiritually drained or empty, even though faith remains. These are some Christians' answers to this feeling:

'I keep on praying regularly, hoping it will pass. It always does.'

'The very act of being still and becoming aware of my feelings, even when they are negative, is worthwhile, so I keep on praying.'

'I try to see if there is anything in my life which might be blocking prayer. I also look back on times when the Lord has been present and know they will return. I try to wait patiently, enduring it with faith and hope and love.'

Here Edwina Gately expresses the same idea:

'Silent God,
empty, sound-less,
like the long dark nights
without life,
I wait, gently hoping for your touch which says,
"I am here".
But the void remains,
Unfilled.
Silent God,
Why do you hide your face
from me?'

I Hear a Seed Growing by Edwina Gately

No experienced Christian would say that life is easy, but they might agree with St Paul's account of Jesus' words:

'My grace is all you need.'

2 Corinthians 12:9

Three centuries ago, a tinker lived in Bedford. His name was John Bunyan. He was a preacher and some Christians who didn't share his ideas threw him into prison. While he was there he wrote a book called *The Pilgrim's Progress*. It is the story of the spiritual journey of a man from the wilderness of this world to the Celestial City. He writes about almost drowning in the Slough of Despond and fighting with Giant Despair, but he has friends who help him – companions like Hopeful and Faithful. Many Christians have found his book very helpful.

Tasks

1. Find out more about icons and the rosary. If possible, ask someone to demonstrate how they are used.

2. Discuss how an artefact or visual aid can assist Christian prayer and meditation.

3. Are there times when you feel drained regarding something in your life (not necessarily something spiritual)? How do you cope? Might the advice in this unit be useful in some way?

A Hindu world

Beginnings

Hindus believe that the universe is created, dissolved into nothingness and re-created over a period of billions of years. One of the oldest Hindu scriptures, the Rig Veda, describes how the universe came into being. In it, a primal cosmic person called Purusha is divided up to become the various parts of the universe:

> 'From his mind the moon was born,
> and from his eye the sun,
> From his mouth Indra and the fire,
> From his breath the wind was born.
> From his navel arose the atmosphere,
> And from his head the sky evolved,
> From his feet the earth, and from his ear
> The cardinal points of the compass:
> So did they fashion forth these worlds.'

Rig Veda, 10, 90

A creation story

There is a story from the scriptures called the Puranas, which describes God's creative powers. It is said that before anything existed, there was only Vishnu, one of the names given to the Supreme Being. The photo shows Vishnu reclining on the body of a mighty serpent.

The story relates how Vishnu, in one corner of a never-ending sky, created a cloud out of

Vishnu reclining on the coils of a serpent

which came a great ocean. On this ocean of eternity Vishnu slept in the coils of a serpent. Through the regular breaths of Vishnu, time came into being. As years passed, the first sound, **aum**, was uttered. Hindus believe this sound is the basis of all life. From aum came the ether (space) and there followed the other four elements, which make up material nature. These elements are air, fire, water and earth.

As Vishnu breathed out, tiny bubbles were scattered into the waters; as Vishnu breathed in, the bubbles were sucked back into him. It is believed that each of these bubbles contains a universe. Vishnu enters each universe and gives it life by filling it with his own spiritual nature – in other words, filling life with souls. In the second part of creation, material life came into being. From Vishnu came Brahma, appearing in the petals of a lotus flower. Brahma was asked to create the planets and stars. It is said that other gods were created and linked to aspects of the universe: Indra to rain, Vayu to wind, Surya the sun, Chandra the moon, Varuna the waters and the goddess Bhumi, who was given charge over the Earth.

As part of a cosmic process of creation, the Earth was filled with all forms of life, including human beings. Hindus believe that all forms of life contain God's spirit. In human beings, this spirit is called the atman. This spirit does not die when the material body dies. The spirit's final goal is to return to God.

Reverence for life

Given the belief that all forms of life have a spiritual basis, Hindus regard the universe as the body of God. It is sometimes said that the Earth's oceans are Vishnu's waist, the hills and mountains his bones, the rivers his veins, the sun and moon his eyes and the trees his hair. The moving of his eyelids marks the passage of day and night. In this sense, Hindus believe that God is everywhere, and that all forms of

Hindus believe that the Earth and life should be respected

life have a soul. All of creation is an expression of the divine spirit – so the Earth and life on it should be respected. Plants, trees, animals and the five natural elements are all related and connected in the rhythm of life. The Earth is often referred to as the 'universal mother'. Part of a hymn in the Atharva Veda says:

> 'O mother, with your oceans, rivers and other bodies of water, you give us land to grow grains, on which our survival depends. Please give us as much milk, fruits, water and cereals as we need to eat and drink.'

Many Hindus are vegetarians for religious reasons. They believe that animals have souls and they should not be killed for food. The cow, especially, is respected as the giver of products which sustain human life.

The five elements of nature are linked to the five senses in human beings: hearing to space, touching to air, sight to fire, taste to water and smell to earth. The daily offering of worship and praise to God includes the use of the natural elements as well as the use of the five human senses. This is a reminder to Hindus that all material nature has sacred origins; and Hindus would say, what better way to praise God than to use material creation, soaked with God's spirit, as part of worship?

Tasks

1 Look at the two Hindu accounts of creation. In what ways do they reflect Hindu beliefs about the sacredness of life?

2 Why do you think a devout Hindu might object to the use of animals for scientific experiments?

3 Imagine a Hindu writing a letter of protest about sea and land pollution. What points would the writer raise and why?

27 Questions of life

Hindus and ultimate questions

All the world's religions have attempted to answer questions about humanity – questions like: 'Who am I?' and 'What is the purpose of life?' Of course some people have provided answers without reference to religions and God. Questions which relate to purpose in life are sometimes called 'ultimate questions'. Hinduism provides a range of answers to such questions. The Upanishads (certain Hindu scriptures) are especially important to Hindus because they provide ideas and record the experiences of ancient holy men who have thought about ultimate questions. The word upanishad means 'to sit down near' a spiritual teacher, much in the way shown in the photo.

Atman and reincarnation

Hindus believe that all forms of life have souls. It is believed that a part of God, **Brahman**, is also present in human beings. This part of God is called the soul or spirit, atman. Hindus believe that the soul lives on when the body dies. The soul takes on another existence in another body. In the Bhagavad Gita, Krishna says:

> 'As a man casts off his worn-out clothes and takes on other new ones, so does the embodied soul cast off its worn-out bodies and enters other new ones.'
>
> Bhagavad Gita 2:22

Belief in the law of karma and reincarnation means that a human will keep returning to life on earth. The new form of life depends on the actions, good and bad, committed in the previous existence. One of the Upanishads explains it like this:

> 'Whatever deeds he does on earth,
> Their rewards he reaps.
> From the other world he comes back here,
> To the world of deed and work.'
>
> Brihadaranyaka Upanishad 4 iv 6

The final goal for Hindus is to be freed from the cycle of birth, death and re-birth. It is believed that this freedom is achieved when humans realize their true spiritual nature; when they are free from desire, greed, hatred and envy; when humans realize their oneness with Brahman.

What is life?

The teachings in the Upanishads and the Bhagavad Gita suggest that human beings have desires which are difficult to overcome. The very fact of existence means that humans need to fulfil desires if they are to survive. Imagine what would happen to a baby if its need for food, warmth and love were denied. Hindus say that there are three characteristics (**gunas**) which influence human thoughts, behaviour and emotions.

These are:

- goodness and light
- passion and energy
- dullness and darkness.

Hindu guru (teacher) with pupil sitting beside him

Difficulties in life occur when passion and darkness begin to dominate. Problems occur when humans begin to think that the fulfilment of physical, mental and emotional needs, at the cost of goodness, is the sum total of existence. Hindus believe that ultimately things of this world are mere reflections or appearances. But humans mistake appearances, which are not permanent, for reality, just as it is easy to imagine in darkness that a piece of rope is a snake. Being fooled, humans can easily become attached to possessions.

What is Brahman?

Hindus believe that only Brahman is ultimately real and everlasting. This is a prayer from the Upanishads which helps Hindus to remember what to strive for in life:

'From the unreal lead me to the real!
From darkness lead me to the light!
From death lead me to immortality!'

Brihadaranyaka Upanishad 1 iii 28

The following is a story from the Chandogya Upanishad.

A boy called Svetaketu goes away to learn from a spiritual teacher at the age of twelve. He returns to his father at the age of twenty-four, thinking that he has learnt the ancient wisdom of the Vedas. His father soon realizes that his son may have learnt the scriptures but he still does not understand the nature of Brahman. So he asks his son to bring a glass of water and to put some salt in it. The following day, Svetaketu is asked to find the salt. But he cannot find it because it has dissolved in the water. The father asks him to sip the water and enquires how it tastes. 'Salty', the young man replies. The father then asks his son to taste the water from the middle of the glass and again from the bottom. 'Where is the salt?' asks the father. 'I cannot see the salt. I only see water', replies Svetaketu. His father then says, 'In the same way, my son, you cannot see the spirit which encompasses the universe. But it is there. That is reality. That is the truth. And you are that truth.'

What is atman?

Many Upanishads teach Hindus that Brahman and the spirit in humans, atman, are connected. Hindus recognize that this relationship is complex. Some would say that Brahman and atman are united; others would say that the two are distinct. But it is agreed that liberation, **moksha**, from the cycle of rebirth is achieved when humans beings realize their oneness with God. Hindus believe that God is like an infinite ocean. Humans with their bodies and minds are like bubbles which get washed up on the shore. It is only when the bubble gets attached to the wave that it becomes aware of its link, its unity with the expanse of the ocean.

'There is a Spirit which is pure and which is beyond old age and death; and beyond hunger and thirst and sorrow. This is Atman, the Spirit in man. All the desires of this Spirit are Truth. It is this Spirit that we must find and know: man must find his own Soul. He who has found and knows his Soul has found all the worlds, has achieved all his desires.'

Chandogya Upanishad 8 vii 1

Tasks

1 With a partner, talk about the Hindu idea of characteristics – the gunas – which, it is believed, influence human activities and emotions. Think about your own feelings and actions. How could these be explained in terms of the gunas?

2 How do you think a Hindu's behaviour is affected by the belief in Brahman and atman?

3 Read the story of Svetaketu and his father. In what ways is it similar to the picture of an infinite ocean and the bubbles in waves? What do you think is the point of the story?

Yoga – the path of knowledge

A yogi who is in deep meditation

Hindus believe that there are three paths to achieving freedom from the cycle of rebirth.The achievement of freedom is called moksha. The paths to freedom are called jnana yoga, karma yoga and bhakti yoga. Each of the these is considered in the next few units.

Yoga

The word yoga comes from a Sanskrit word yuj, which means 'to unite' or 'to join together'. The origin of the word 'religion' has much the same meaning: 'to bind together'. Yoga sets out to unite the different aspects of a person – to unite the human and the divine. In the West, yoga is often presented as a series of weird and wonderful physical exercises. Sometimes, the divine element is neglected altogether. It is also true to say that in some aspects of Hindu philosophy, yoga can be practised without reference to a loving God.

Yoga, as described in the Indian book the Yogasutra, identifies eight steps or 'limbs'. The first limb is about avoiding negative things such as violence, falsehood, theft and greed. The second limb requires people to develop positive aspects such as purity and self-discipline. Awareness of God being everywhere and in everything, as well as loving God, are important here, too. The third limb is concerned with right postures – **asana**, for example: sitting correctly, which should make one alert and relaxed. The fourth limb considers proper breathing, allowing people to concentrate without distraction. The fifth limb is turning the senses inward, switching the mind off from outside influences. The sixth limb involves mastering concentration so that the mind is bound to a single object of attention. The seventh limb is meditation, when there is an uninterrupted flow of attention to the mind. The last limb is called samadhi. This is a state of silence or self-realization. Sometimes it is referred to as a state of 'pure seeing', of insight and illumination – a state of higher consciousness, which is not sensual or mental in the ordinary sense, but more like mystical insight. The first few of the limbs can help as preparation for the others. But the steps do not necessarily follow one after the other like steps on a ladder. It could be that a person does not become wise by breathing, sitting or thinking in a particular way; the person might breathe and think in that way because the person is wise.

Jnana yoga

The word jnana means 'knowledge'. Hindu teachings distinguish between 'rational knowledge' (for example, knowing how the body works) and 'spiritual knowledge'. The purpose of spiritual knowledge is to understand, through experience, that human beings are a part of, or at one with, the Supreme Being.

Both men and women can practise yoga. A female practitioner is called a yogini and a male practitioner is called a yogi. The practice of jnana yoga, as outlined in the Bhagavad Gita, seeks to achieve oneness with God, in the form of Krishna. Hindus believe that Vishnu appears in many forms, including the deity Krishna, who came to Earth to destroy evil and to restore goodness. Krishna's teachings are contained in the Bhagavad Gita. In one of its sections, Krishna describes to his friend Arjun how a person can control the mind and achieve peace:

'Let him set up for himself a steady seat in a clean place, neither too high nor yet too low, bestrewn with cloth or hide or grass.

There let him sit and make his mind a single point, let him restrain the operations of his thought and senses and concentrate on spiritual exercise to purify the self.

Remaining still, let him keep body, head, and neck in a straight line, unmoving; let him fix his eye on the tip of his nose, not looking round about him.

There let him sit, self all stilled, his fear all gone, firm in his vow of chastity, his mind controlled, his thoughts on Me, integrated, yet intent on Me.

Thus let the athlete of the spirit be constant in integrating himself, his mind restrained; then will he approach that peace ... which lives in Me.'

Bhagavad Gita 6:10–15

Tasks

1   What physical and mental qualities would a Hindu practitioner of jnana yoga need to develop? What sorts of difficulties would she or he have to overcome to control the mind and the body?

2   Hindus say that regular meditation helps them to 'communicate' with the 'inner self'. What do you think is meant by this? How might a Hindu's daily life be affected by regular meditation?

3   Think about the times you are still and silent. How does this compare with the techniques of a yogi or yogini?

4   Some Hindus in India become 'sannyasins'. This means that they give up all their possessions and family attachments. Much of their time is spent on meditation. With a partner, discuss the benefits and disadvantages in life for a Hindu who has become a sannyasin.

Yoga – the path of unselfish action

In one of the Hindu scriptures, it is said that:

> 'As a man acts (karma), as he behaves, so does he become. Whoso does good, becomes good: whoso does evil, becomes evil. By good works a man becomes holy, by evil works he becomes evil ...'

Brihadaranyaka Upanishad 4 iv 5

The importance of work

Hindus often use the word **dharma** to describe their religion. This word can mean several things, including 'duty'. Good Hindus try to carry out their duties, which vary according to their ages and their positions in the family and community and as individuals. Service (seva) towards others is highly valued. Along with this idea of service goes the notion of sacrifice. Daily work should be done without thought for reward. Selfless service counts for more than work done from greed and desire.

Hindus recognize that the fact of existing means that humans are bound up with the sense of self and all its desires. This is explained by the three gunas, the characteristics, or strands, which are part of the make-up of humans and material nature. Hindus believe that the strand of goodness causes the self to cling to joy and wisdom; the strand of passion clings to activity and pleasures, but can also bring pain; darkness clings to dullness and ignorance. If humans are so bound, Hindu teachings ask, what opportunities are there for release?

Karma yoga

The Bhagavad Gita explains that performing work, karma yoga, without seeking rewards in return, can help a Hindu to achieve liberation.

> 'On Me alone let your mind dwell, stir up your soul to enter Me; thenceforth in very truth in Me you will find your home.
> But if you are unable in all your steadfastness to concentrate your thoughts on Me, then seek to win Me by effort unremitting.
> And if for such effort you lack the strength, then work-and-act for me, make this your goal; for even if you work only for my sake, you will receive the prize.
> And then again if even this exceeds your powers, gird up your loins, renounce the fruit of all your works with self restraint.
> For better is wisdom than effort, better than wisdom meditation; and better than meditation to renounce the fruit of works: renunciation leads straightway to peace.'

Bhagavad Gita 12:8–12

Gandhi: an example of unselfish action

One of the most famous Hindus of modern times is Mohandas Gandhi. He has been called the 'saint of action'. Hindus gave him the title 'Mahatma', meaning 'great soul'. He was a man of high principles who lived them out in his daily life. For example, the photograph shows him with a spinning wheel. This was his way of saying to Indians that they should be self-reliant, without having to import goods from other countries. Gandhi also believed that God and Truth were the same. He used this belief to develop the idea of satyagrahya, meaning 'the force of truth'. This force of truth was used by Gandhi and his followers as a non-violent way **(ahimsa)** of achieving social and political justice. Gandhi was a great admirer of the Bhagavad Gita and found a lot in the teachings of Krishna to inspire and guide him in his daily actions. Here are two examples of Gandhi's thoughts and experiences. In a letter to an English friend Gandhi wrote:

Gandhi working at a spinning wheel

'The purpose of life is undoubtedly to know oneself. We cannot do it unless we learn to identify ourselves with all that lives. The sum total of that life is God. The instrument of this knowledge is boundless, selfless service.'

Gandhi wrote about his experience of God:

'Like a voice from afar and yet quite near. It was as unmistakable as some human voice ... The hearing of the voice was preceded by a terrific struggle within me. Suddenly the voice came upon me. I listened, made certain it was the voice, and the struggle ceased. I was calm ... not the unanimous verdict of the whole world against me could shake me from the belief that what I heard was the voice of God.'

The importance of Gandhi to Hindus and others is that he stands out as an example of someone whose spirituality was turned into selfless and sacrificial action: for the poor, the hungry and the outcast, as well as for the rights of Indians to achieve independence from British rule.

Tasks

1   Why do you think Gandhi has been described as the 'saint of action'?

2   Think about times when you have performed works or actions without thinking about their rewards. Was it easy or hard?

3   Hindus would say that their belief in God has to be shown in everyday life, through their actions. Some Hindus would say that, in the end, it is not what a person thinks or says that matters as much as what the person does. How would Hindus who hold this view argue their case?

Yoga – the path of loving devotion

Bhakti yoga

Throughout the ages, Hindus have worshipped God in different forms and in different ways. Hindus see this variety as expressing the wide range of meaning which is in God. Of the three paths to achieving moksha, the path of love and devotion directed towards God is the most popular. Loving devotion or bhakti, can be expressed through worship, dance and the performing arts, expressive arts such as painting and sculpture and the literary arts. The main forms of devotion in Hinduism are directed towards the reincarnations of God in the forms of Rama, Krishna and Shiva. Many Hindus have a chosen deity, an ishtadevata. This chosen form of God can be a personal or a family deity. Directing love and devotion to a deity, bhakti yoga, is one way for Hindus to express their faith in God.

When Hindus think of God as having form and qualities, it helps them to direct their worship and devotion. Often deities are pictured in male and female forms. Goddesses symbolize the energy of God, shakti, and gods have female consorts. For example, Shiva is linked to the goddess Parvati, who is also worshipped as the goddess Durga and the fierce Kali. Vishnu is linked to Lakshmi, the goddess of good fortune. In the picture is the deity Krishna, who is linked to Radha. Another example is Sita, who remains dutiful and loyal to Rama while in captivity.

Hindus who follow the path of bhakti yoga try to express their love for God by following the example set by Rama and Sita. Hindus believe the love Radha and the milk maids (gopis) showed for Krishna, is a symbol of the love that God has for his worshippers. They believe the expression of bhakti is deep and profound. It is a trusting and faithful kind of love, not desiring favours in return. It may seem like the love shown through human relationships, such as the love between parents and children,

Krishna and Radha, symbolizing the love God has for his worshippers

but the expression of love directed towards God is pure and perfect. In other words, bhakti yoga is God-centred and not self-centred.

The Bhagavad Gita's teaching on bhakti yoga

The Bhagavad Gita is one of the most important scriptures in modern Hinduism. It was composed around 2,000 years ago. For many Hindus the Bhagavad Gita is a source of inspiration and a guide for daily behaviour. Most Hindus, in practice, do not follow just one of the three paths. Devout Hindus meditate, worship and perform good works without desiring rewards. This is a way of expressing Hindus' love for God. In the Bhagavad Gita, Krishna explains to his friend Arjun the value of a person who achieves peace and tranquillity through meditation and self-control. Although the words in the following quotes refer to a male, the teachings of Krishna are directed to both men and women.

> 'Only the man who remains in this world and, before he is released from the body, can stand fast against the onset of desire and anger, is truly integrated, truly happy. His joy within, his bliss within, his light within, the man who is integrated in spiritual exercise becomes Brahman ...'

Bhagavad Gita 5:23–4

In a later section, Krishna praises a 'spiritual athlete':

> 'With self integrated by spiritual exercise, he sees the self in all beings standing, all beings in the self: the same in everything he sees. Who sees Me everywhere, who sees the All in Me, for him I am not lost, nor is he lost to Me.'

Bhagavad Gita 6:29–30

Krishna explains to Arjuna that the paths to God are difficult because the mind is fickle and hard to control. Human beings can easily be led astray by desire and greed. But if a devotee learns self-control and also develops love for Krishna, that devotee can achieve freedom from the cycle of rebirth and death.

> 'When a man dwells in the solitude of silence, and meditation and contemplation are ever with him; when too much food does not disturb his health, and his thoughts and words and body are in peace; when freedom from passion is his constant will;
> And his selfishness and violence and pride are gone; when lust and anger and greediness are no more, and he is free from the thought "this is mine"; then this man has risen on the mountain of the Highest: he is

worthy to be one with Brahman, with God. He is one with Brahman, with God, and beyond grief and desire his soul is in peace. His love is one for all creation, and he has supreme love for me.
By love he knows me in truth, who I am and what I am. And when he knows me in truth he enters into my Being.'

Bhagavad Gita 18:52–5

Hindus believe that in whatever form and whatever way they choose to worship God, the idea that the spirit of God is reflected in humanity and in all creation should direct their thoughts, deeds and love.

Tasks

1 Look at the illustration of Krishna and Radha. What characteristics do they show for Hindus?

2 For many Hindus the path of bhakti is an important way of worshipping and showing devotion to God. Identify the ways in which bhakti is translated into action by Hindus.

3 What do you think a Hindu gains by following the path of bhakti? What kinds of emotions might be experienced?

Pilgrimage

An important part of being a devout Hindu is to make a religious journey: a pilgrimage. Hindus call this yatra. Although pilgrimage is not compulsory, Hindus see it as an important part of their spiritual development. Making a journey, often over long distances and involving hardships, helps a pilgrim to grow in inner strength. It is also a way of showing love for God. In India, pilgrimages are made by individuals as well as by groups or even whole villages. Hindus from other parts of the world also make pilgrimage journeys to India.

Sites of pilgrimage

Many parts of India are regarded as sacred places. Indeed, for many Hindus, the whole country is believed to be holy. Some special destinations become very crowded, especially at festival times. Among the popular destinations

are mountains (such as the Himalayas), temples and rivers. Some pilgrims include the four 'abodes' or homes of God as their destinations. These are believed to be at the four compass points: Badrinath in the north, Puri in the east, Dwarka in the west and Ramesvaram in the south. All these places have shrines dedicated to Hindu gods and goddesses, where pilgrims go to make offerings and to experience the power and feelings of being in the presence of God.

Reasons for going on a yatra

Hindus go on pilgrimage for many reasons. A family member could be fulfilling a vow made to a chosen deity, for blessings of good health, thanksgiving for the birth of a baby and as an act of worship and devotion to God. Yatra is also performed to gain religious merit. The final aim in life for a Hindu is to seek release from the cycle of death and rebirth. Hindus believe that by going on a pilgrimage, they can replace the past and present results of bad deeds with good deeds and merit, as long as they are sincere. It also gives the chance for **darshan.** This means being in the presence of God, 'seeing' the divine in the form of an image or **murti** in a temple, and being blessed.

Bathing in sacred rivers

Hindus believe that there are seven sacred rivers. Of these, the most sacred is the Ganga. Where rivers cross, it is regarded as a more special place to bathe. For example, where the rivers Ganga and Yumuna meet and flow together at Prayag (Allahabad), ritual bathing is believed to wash away sins and to help gain religious merit called punya.

Hindus regard fords or crossing places **(tirtha)** as spiritual gateways. Fords enable people to cross safely from one side to another. In a symbolic way a tirtha enables believers to cross over from the cycle of samsara to spiritual freedom. This is why bathing in the Ganga and

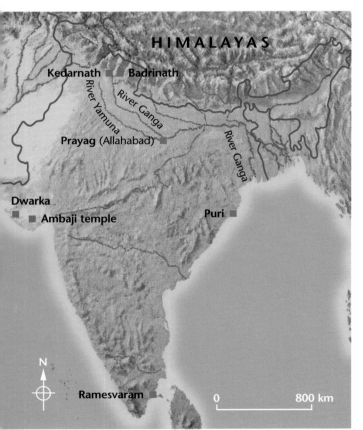

Map of India showing some of the holy sites and rivers

Pilgrims bathing in the River Ganga

scattering a dead person's cremated ashes on this river is regarded as special by devout Hindus.

Climbing hills and mountains

The Himalayas are famous pilgrimage sites. Mount Kailasha, in the central Himalayas, is believed to be the abode of the deity Shiva. Hindu pilgrims make long and difficult journeys to hilltop shrines, such as Badrinath and Kedarnath in the Himalayan foothills. One of the highlights for a pilgrim after arriving at the temples and shrines is to bow down in front of the murtis and obtain darshan, to be in the presence of God.

This is how one pilgrim describes his experience of yatra:

'This time, my journey was to the hilltop temple of the goddess Ambaji in Gujarat. I was with a group of others and we had to climb 9,999 steps. The first few thousand steps seemed easy enough. We sang bhajans (hymns) praising God and it felt good to be with other devotees. We also talked about our difficulties in life: the pains of ill-health, the misfortunes of work and past quarrels with friends and family members. It is remarkable how universal suffering is, whether you come from a village, a town or a city. Sharing experiences ▶

▶ of suffering and of the joys in life with fellow pilgrims began to give me a sense of unity. As we talked more about what really matters in life, our devotion to God, my faith increased with every difficult step. My whole body ached as we climbed higher and higher, but I kept reciting my favourite prayer, called the Gayatri Mantra, and I felt strengthened: "Let us meditate on the Divine Source of Light; May it illuminate our thoughts and prayers". When we eventually arrived at the shrine of Ambaji at the top, I felt exhilarated! Taking darshan and offering my flowers at the shrine sparked indescribable joy and peace within me. This sense of oneness with God I treasure in my daily life, even now, many years later.'

Tasks

1   Hindus would say that they go on pilgrimages to gain spiritual strength. What do you think they mean by this? How do you think they achieve this goal?

2   Imagine you are a Hindu who has just been on pilgrimage to a site in India. Explain to a friend how it affected you. You can do this as a letter, a poem or an illustration.

Symbols of spirituality

A Hindu swastika marked on the side of a building

Followers of all religions use signs and symbols to describe their faith. Sometimes, signs and icons are used to assist worship. They help to focus the mind and heart on the object of worship and adoration. Hindus use a variety of symbols and words as aids for meditation and worship. The purpose of these aids is to help a Hindu to concentrate and to help gain greater spiritual consciousness.

The swastika

This powerful ancient symbol, 4,000 years old, is a four-sided cross. Swastika literally means 'it is well'. It is the symbol of good fortune, an ancient sun sign with right-angled arms. These stand for the indirect way that God can be understood – not so much by intellectual reasoning as by intuition and experience. It is ironic that Hitler's fascist party used the swastika in a negative way, so that in many people's minds the symbol awakens memories of destruction. Hindus still use the symbol as a sign for well-being and good fortune.

The lotus flower

The lotus flower, called a padma, is a symbol of the universe and humanity. The flower itself is an example of perfection and great beauty. Its roots grow in muddy waters, hidden from the eyes, so that only the beauty is visible.

The roots in muddy water represent material life and ignorance; the flower on the water, opening to the sky, symbolizes the spiritual being. The lotus flower is associated with the goddess Lakshmi.

Prayer beads

Beads threaded together to form a **mala** (rosary) are used by devotees as an aid to concentration. The beads may be made from seeds or sandalwood. Seeds called rudraksha are highly regarded as the compassionate tears which the deity Shiva shed for humankind's suffering. Followers of Shiva wear malas made of such seeds as a symbol of God's love. During worship or meditation, Shiva's name is chanted: 'Aum Namah Shivaya', as the devotee passes each bead through the finger and thumb. Devotees of other deities use a mala during worship and meditation.

Use of a mantra

A **mantra** is a formula of sacred words. It is a verbal aid used to assist meditation. Sometimes a mantra is given by a spiritual teacher (a guru) to a student. It has to be repeated over and over again so that it helps to focus the mind on a single aspect. The very sound of the words can help make people conscious of their inner spirit. For example, devotees of Krishna or Shiva often chant a mantra over and over again as a way of praising their chosen deity.

A lotus flower in blossom is a sign of perfection and purity

A yantra helps worshippers to concentrate on God

The sacred symbol OM representing the sound of God

Yantra

A yantra is an abstract picture or a diagram that represents a deity. The design can be geometric and the colours symbolize the nature of the deity being worshipped. A yantra is used by a worshipper to control the mind and to prevent thoughts from wandering.

Aum

The sacred symbol aum (sometimes spelt 'om') has many deep meanings for a Hindu. It represents the sound of God: 'Brahman as sound'. It is also the symbol of creation and stands for life, death and the after-life. The three parts of the symbol also represent the three states of consciousness in humans: being awake, dreaming and dreamless sleep. Aum is the whole universe, its beginning and its end. The syllable is chanted at the beginning and at the end of all prayers and worship.

For Hindus, reciting the sacred syllable aum can enable a person to reach the soundless, silent Brahman. The following verse from a Hindu scripture helps to bring out the profound meaning of the sacred syllable:

'OM. In the centre of the castle of Brahman, our own body, there is a small shrine in the form of a lotus flower, and within it can be found a small space. We should find who dwells there and we should want to know him.

And if anyone asks: "Who is he who dwells in a small shrine in the form of a lotus flower in the centre of the castle of Brahman? Whom shall we want to find and know?"

We can answer: "The little space within the heart is as great as this vast universe. The heavens and the earth are there, and the sun, and the moon, and the stars; fire and lightning and the winds are there; and all that now is and all that is not; for the whole universe is in Him and He dwells within our heart."'

Chandogya Upanishad 8 i 1–3

Tasks

1 Look at and concentrate on the picture of the yantra shown here, or design your own yantra. What thoughts and feelings does it conjure up for you?

2 Study the verse which appears with the Hindu sacred syllable aum. What does it tell you about a Hindu's belief in God?

3 What does a Hindu's use of symbols and mantras tell you about Hindu spirituality?

33 Allah's revelation

Introduction

The Islamic faith has at its centre an overwhelming belief (**tawhid**) in the one God who created the universe. Throughout the world, Muslims prefer to use the Arabic word, Allah, for God. This is a word without a plural or a feminine form. Allah is unlike anything within human experience. He is contained by nothing, not even the universe itself. However, despite his great majesty, he is seen as being close to humanity and prepared to grant people's requests.

To Muslims the worship of Allah lies at the heart of their faith, while tawhid is the reason for every action. Whenever Muslims do something, they call on Allah's assistance, often with the phrase 'Bismillah-ir-Rahman-ir-Rahim' – 'In the name of God, the Gracious, the Merciful'. These are the words which begin every chapter of the **Qur'an.**

The name of Allah is often beautifully decorated

The Qur'an

Muslims have a special place in their hearts for the Qur'an, for it records the words of Allah, dictated by the angel **Jibril** to the Prophet Muhammad (**PBUH**). The Qur'an is often referred to as the Furqan – the Discernment – because it distinguishes between right and wrong. As well as giving powerful descriptions of heaven and hell, it is a history of the long battle between good and evil.

Muslims believe that without the explanations given by Allah, human beings cannot know why they were created. The Qur'an tells us that we were created by Allah to be his representatives on Earth. In order to carry out these duties the human race was given certain features. These include freedom of action and the human soul (ruh). Although we all have this soul, which helps us to survive difficulties, appreciate life and act creatively, we do not really understand what it is. For Muslims there is no better description than the following Qur'anic verse:

> 'They ask you concerning
> The spirit.
> Say: "The spirit is of the
> Command of my Lord
> Only a little knowledge
> Of it is communicated
> To you."'

> Qur'an 17:85

While all human beings must have a soul in order to carry out their duties on Earth, it isn't necessary for us to understand what it is or how it works. We can all use video-recorders, but very few of us know exactly how they work, and it is the same with the human soul. We know that we have one, for it allows us to think and to be what we are, and we are often advised to get the most out of having a soul. However, Muslims believe that this Qur'anic verse is a reminder that our understanding is limited and humanity has only been taught about a part of Allah's creation.

By reading the Qur'an a Muslim is drawn closer to Allah

Reciting the Qur'an

The Qur'an occupies a unique position in the life of Muslims because they believe that it contains the actual words of Allah. There are numerous **hadith** – records of the words of the Prophet Muhammad (PBUH) – which encourage the reading of the Qur'an, its memorization and its recitation.

Muslims usually spend part of every day reading the Qur'an. It is an activity that brings them very close to Allah. When the Qur'an is read out loud or used in prayer, it is always in Arabic. Although it is best that the meaning be understood, Muslims believe that a spiritual reward is given even when it is recited without understanding. This is because the Qur'an contains Allah's words and it encourages all who hear it to worship him.

Abu Musa Ashari narrated that the Prophet Muhammad (PBUH) said:

'... the case of a Muslim who studies the Holy Qur'an is like the orange which is aromatic and sweet, and the example of a Muslim who does not recite the Holy Qur'an is like a dry date which has no smell but is sweet. And the case of a hypocrite who recites the Holy Qur'an is like the fruit which, although scented, yet tastes bitter, and the case of a hypocrite who does not recite the Holy Qur'an is like the fruit which has no aroma and is bitter in taste.'

Hadith Bukhari and Muslim

Tasks

1 Muslims use the Arabic name for God, which does not have a female or plural form. How might this affect them? Might their opinions differ from your own?

2 Discuss in a small group how important it would be for you to understand all the reasons for something you are asked to do. Do you have to understand everything? Or do you just need to know what you have to do? Consider the two examples in the text: the video-recorder and the human soul.

34 Important Islamic beliefs

The five pillars

Islam seeks to help the whole person as he or she travels through life. It seeks to support the human body and its soul. Islam is built on five 'pillars' (arkan), or principles, set out in the Prophetic Hadith.

Abdullah bin Umar narrated that the messenger of Allah (PBUH) said:

> '... the structure of Islam is raised on five (pillars), testifying that there is no god but Allah, that Muhammad (PBUH) is his slave and messenger, and the establishment of prayer, payment of zakah, pilgrimage to the House (Kaaba) and the fast of Ramadan.'
>
> Hadith Muslim

The five pillars listed in this hadith are: the statement of faith; prayer; fasting; helping the poor, and the pilgrimage. Each of these helps Muslims to develop their faith.

The statement of faith (shahadah)

The **shahadah** is the first of the five pillars of Islam. It is a simple summary of the Islamic faith in two parts: 'There is no god but Allah and Muhammad (PBUH) is the prophet of Allah'. The first part acknowledges the unique divinity of one god – Allah – while the second links Muslims together with its declaration that Muhammad (PBUH) is the Prophet. The shahadah is a part of the first words that a new-born Muslim baby hears as the call to prayer (**adhan**) is whispered into its right ear. The shahadah is also the declaration that an adult makes on converting to Islam.

The first part of the shahadah is shared with believers of other faiths. It separates Muslims from belief in other gods, including the inanimate beings that previous generations worshipped. The earlier prophets' struggles against this form of idolatry are described in the Qur'an. The stories of young Ibrahim's conflict with his idol-worshipping father and the struggles of Musa, his brother Harun (PBUT) and their people are especially appealing to young people. The rejection of idol-worship in the shahadah also extends to more modern temptations, such as greed and the worship of pop 'idols'. With the statement 'there is no god but Allah', Muslims cleanse their hearts of greed and avarice and open them to the worship of God.

The second part of the shahadah is a positive declaration. It declares that the believer shares the Muslim belief in the prophethood of Muhammad (PBUH). In a religious context this is important because it has preserved the clear distinction between Allah and humanity. All human beings, even the prophets, serve Allah.

The shahadah is often used to decorate mosques; this photograph was taken in Spain

The prophets

Muslims try to model themselves on the Prophet Muhammad (PBUH)'s life. This follows the Prophet's instructions, made during his last pilgrimage: 'I am leaving you with the Book of Allah and the Sunnah of his Prophet. If you follow them, you will never go astray…'.

The Prophet Muhammad (PBUH)'s words and actions have been recorded in great detail. The Qur'an contains descriptions of the lives and patterns of worship of the earlier prophets recommended to Muhammad (PBUH). One of the shortest but most beautiful descriptions applies to the Prophet Yahya, who is known in English as John the Baptist. It is found in Surah Maryam (the Qur'an is divided into 114 surahs, or sections), and some of the description is also used by the Prophet **Isa** (Jesus) about himself later in the surah:

Allah is the centre of a Muslim's worship

> '"O Yahya! take hold
> Of the Book with might":
> And we gave him Wisdom
> Even as a young man,
>
> And (we gave him) pity (for all creatures)
> As from us, and purity:
> He was devout,
>
> And (we made him) kind to his parents,
> And he was not overbearing or rebellious.
>
> So Peace on him
> The day he was born,
> The day that he dies,
> And the day that he
> Will be raised up
> To life (again)!'

Qur'an 19: 12–15

When the Muslims who sought refuge in Abyssinia were pursued by the idol-worshipping Arabs, they recited this surah to support their plea for asylum. It played a n important part in convincing the Christian Negus to let them remain in exile, and it is still a source of inspiration to Muslims in the modern world.

Tasks

1. The statement of faith are the first words that a baby born to Muslim parents hears. Muslims try to say them again just before they die. Choose a person involved on either of these occasions and describe the effect the shahadah might have on them.

2. Choose a person you admire and list all the details you know of their life. In a small group decide whether each detail is one which is worth imitating or not.

3. Draw a mosque with five pillars. Label these: 'shahadah', 'prayer', 'fasting', 'zakah' and 'pilgrimage'. On the dome of the mosque write 'Islam'.

35 Formal prayer – salah

Salah

The second pillar of Islam is the performance of the ritual prayer, or salah. Although praying regularly may become routine, it keeps spiritual communication with Allah open, so that the worshipper can strengthen his or her faith when necessary. Salah consists of a series of actions, linked to recitations from the Qur'an. Muslims normally pray at least five times in each 24 hours. One hadith, narrated by Tirmidhi, tells us that the Prophet said that the difference between believing (**iman**) and not believing (**kufr**) was leaving out the ritual prayer.

Muslims feel that this constant awareness of Allah helps to prevent them from committing sins. While in prayer, Muslims join with the rest of creation in the praise of their Lord. This is when they are most at rest and most at peace with the world.

The nature of salah

Prayer lies at the spiritual centre of Islam. It is the time when a Muslim stands before Allah and communicates with him. Worshipping Allah as though he can be seen is considered to be the most sincere form of worship. It is described as 'excellence' (ihsan).

Prayer begins with the worshipper standing with bent head, reciting the first surah of the Qur'an. This has three elements: acknowledgment of Allah's superiority; the worshipper's commitment to Allah, and a call for assistance. After the first surah, another

Prayer is an oasis of peace in a busy day

short part of the Qur'an is recited, chosen by the worshipper. The worshipper then bows down, and after standing upright, places his or her head on the ground in sujud, assuming the lowest position before Allah. The instructions for this part of prayer are found in the Qur'an:

> 'But celebrate the praises
> Of your Lord and be of those
> Who prostrate themselves
> In adoration.'

Quran 15:98

These movements are repeated a set number of times during each prayer. The prayer ends with greetings to the angels who surround the worshipper. Regular prayer is a vital part of a Muslim's life, but it can only represent the inner prayer which is offered by the devout worshipper to Allah.

The group prayer

Ritual daily prayers may be performed alone or within a group, within a building or in the open air, in a busy market-place or in a secluded garden. While individual prayer is a unique and personal experience, prayer within a group brings another dimension into the relationship with Allah. Muslims do not live alone but in a community. Prayers offered shoulder to shoulder with those viewed as brothers and sisters help to bind the population together. Praying the obligatory prayers with others, whether at home or in the mosque, is strongly recommended by the tradition (sunnah) of the Prophet Muhammad (PBUH). This is widely practised in the congregational prayers performed five times a day in mosques and other public places all over the world. As well as this, one day each week is set aside as the Day of Congregation. On Fridays, Muslims meet together in large, district mosques to pray the noon prayer together and to listen to a sermon on a contemporary spiritual issue.

Sunnah prayers

In addition to their daily prayers, many Muslims also follow the practice of the Prophet Muhammad (PBUH) and offer extra sunnah prayers. For many Muslims, these prayers reinforce their relationship with Allah. They are often performed at times when the soul can relate to the spiritual world: for example, late at night.

Muslims who wish to travel still further along the spiritual path to their creator will offer even more prayers than those recommended by the sunnah of the Prophet. This is because Muslims believe that Allah will respond to their devotions. The following hadith explains that whenever worshippers try to come closer to Allah, Allah will bring them even closer to him. In this hadith Allah's words are spoken in the first person:

> 'And if he draws near to me by a hand's span, I draw near to him by an arm's length; and if he draws near to me by an arm's length, I draw near to him a fathom's length; and if he comes to me walking, I race to him.'

Qudsi Hadith Muslim

Tasks

1   How might the physical movements of salah, for example sujud (shown in the photograph), affect a Muslim's relationship with Allah?

2   Discuss in a small group how you feel when you ask someone for help. Do you feel differently when they actually do more than you asked?

3   Think about the differences in worshipping in a group or alone. List the advantages of each way of worshipping.

36 Informal prayer

Supplication (du'a)

As well as regular prayer (salah), Muslims also offer personal prayers, or **du'a**. This Arabic term for the personal prayer is best translated as 'supplication', or 'a plea'. It was the practice of all the prophets and is recommended by the Quran:

> 'Then, supplicate Allah
> With sincere devotion to Him,
> Even though the Unbelievers
> May detest it.'
>
> Qur'an 40:14

Du'a may be a practical request, or a plea for the blessings (**barakah**) of Allah. Asking Allah for something is an important part of worship. The person asking for the favour knows Allah's power, but also knows that the request may not be granted, because Allah knows best where someone's destiny lies.

A supplication to Allah may be made in any language, although it is recommended that Muslims learn the supplications of the Qur'an. A supplication may be made secretly, in the heart of the believer, or voiced very quietly, for Allah is always near. While it is natural for the human soul to call on him in times of need, it is equally important to communicate with Allah in times of peace. Certain times are considered to be especially appropriate: the later part of the night, the Friday of every week, every **Ramadan** (see page 76) and the part of the pilgrimage spent at **Arafat** (see pages 78–9).

Allah as the controller of destiny

A Muslim student describes how believing that Allah controls human destiny has shaped her attitude to life:

> 'I have always found it very helpful to know that Allah will help me do what is best for me. For example, I always want to do well ▶ in my exams. But after I've revised as much as I can, I make du'a and leave the rest to Allah. If he wants me to fail and do something else with my life then that is the best result. I still don't enjoy exams, but when I see how nervous my friends are then I know I am really fortunate because the trust I have in Allah lets me do so much better than I deserve.'

Remembrance of Allah (dhikr)

Another way Muslims worship Allah is by repeating his name. The Arabic name for this repetition is **dhikr**. A hadith explaining how this should be done was narrated by Kab bin Ujrah, who tells us that the Prophet Muhammad (PBUH) said:

> 'There are phrases which, if recited after every prescribed prayer, will cause a person never to be disappointed. That is to say, "Subhan Allah" ("Praise be to Allah") 33 times, "Al-hamdu-li-Llah" ("Thanks to Allah") 33 times and "Allahu akbar" ("Allah is great") 34 times.'
>
> Hadith Muslim

Muslims remember Allah by repeating his name

This calling on Allah is often performed after prayer. It may be done by an individual or in a group. If worshippers want to repeat the phrases 100 times, they can use the finger joints of the right hand to count 33 three times, as the Prophet used to do; or they can use a **tasbih** of 33 or 99 beads, as shown in the photograph. Both these methods of counting may also be used to recall the 99 different attributes of Allah mentioned in the Qur'an.

The Sufi movement

There are many hadith which encourage Muslims to remember Allah. The Sufi orders base their spiritual practices on these hadith. These orders are formal gatherings of Muslims who have a more spiritual inclination or who feel the need of greater purification. They usually gather after Friday prayer or in the evening between **Maghrib** and **Isha** prayers. They meet in the mosque, in the open air or in the home of one of the group.

The Sufi movement traces its origins back to the **ahl-al-suffah**, who were among the companions of the Prophet Muhammad (PBUH). During the second century of Islam **Sufism** emerged as an organized movement within Islam. Sufism is a strongly spiritual movement. Its members practise voluntary prayers, fasts, du'a and Qur'anic recitation. All Sufi groups believe that dhikr concentrates the heart and mind on the worship of Allah. The particular form of dhikr varies between the groups, and this is the most distinctive practice of each Sufi order.

Muslims who have felt attracted to the Sufi movement have often had a very spiritual understanding of Islam, and this has helped to maintain Islamic customs and traditions. The Sufi orders were especially important when Muslim countries were colonized by European powers. Then the Sufi orders played an important role as a safe haven of the faith.

Sufi orders may meet in the home of one of the group

Tasks

1 Can everyone always have what they want? Is it possible? What happens if people's wishes clash?

2 In a small group discuss the different ways you have of relaxing. How many of them involve repetitive actions?

3 To count to 33 when performing dhikr, Muslims use the fingers of one hand. To show how this is done, draw round your left hand. This will look like your right hand palm up. Starting at the top joint of the smallest finger, write 1, 2 and 3 down the smallest finger; then 4, 5 and 6 on the next finger. Continue in this way with 13, 14 and 15 down the thumb. Go back to the little finger to start again with 16, 17 and 18, and continue until you reach 31 32 and 33, which are also written on the smallest finger.

37 | Fasting and charity

Fasting

Many religions have a custom of giving up food for a while in order to concentrate on more important matters. If people fast during the day, their daily routine is abandoned and all their energy is channelled to spiritual activity. Many people see this as a time when the spirit tames the body.

As well as Ramadan (see below), many Muslims try to fast in one of the different ways that the Prophet Muhammad (PBUH) used to fast. Some people fast on the middle three days of the **lunar month;** others fast each Monday and Thursday, and others fast on alternate days. The Prophet Muhammad (PBUH) did not allow more fasting than this as it would be unfair to family and friends.

Ramadan

Muslims look forward to Ramadan, a month when Allah's blessings are given to people. Fasting is not seen as a punishment, and some people are unable to fast. Young children would find it too hard, and they do not need to fast until they are about thirteen. Those who are ill or away from home can break their fast and make up the missed days after the month, and people who are too old to fast can donate food to the poor instead.

Fasting is much more than not eating or drinking during the day. It is a period of total physical and emotional cleansing, like training for a sporting event. People give up everything they want, because they know that winning will make them feel so good. By fasting, the mind controls the body, and this feeling of control ensures that people will not be tempted to misbehave ever again.

The fasting Muslim should also try to avoid conflict with others, reminding them, if necessary, that they are fasting. In this way Ramadan becomes a month of harmony and goodwill among the Muslim community. The ultimate goal of fasting is to liberate the human soul from all worldly worries, developing a complete lack of concern for anything but Allah and the hereafter. Having attained this state of trust in Allah, worries such as how or where the fast will be broken become irrelevant.

Breaking the fast with others is recommended and, all over the world, Muslims gather in each other's homes or in mosques to celebrate the completion of another day's fast and to pray for its acceptance.

Here a Muslim describes the way Ramadan is different from the rest of the year:

'Just like every other Muslim, I look forward to Ramadan. It is a milestone in the year. We always wonder how we will cope with the trials of fasting, but are surprised every year how easy it is. We even sometimes wonder whether we even need to start to eat normally again! Then, after it's gone, we feel sad. It's another year to wait for that special feeling to return.'

Itikaf

The other activity of Ramadan is the retreat **(itikaf).** This happens during the last ten days

Itikaf gives the Muslim time to concentrate on worshipping Allah

Giving money to the poor at the end of Ramadan allows everyone to enjoy the festivities

of Ramadan, for it was on one of these nights that the Qur'an was first revealed to Muhammad (PBUH). When practising itikaf, a man withdraws from normal activities and stays in the mosque, ideally for the whole of the ten days, leaving it only if absolutely necessary. He sleeps in the mosque and devotes all his waking time to prayer, reading the Quran, du'a and dhikr. For him it is an almost unique time to stand back from the stresses of normal life and to devote himself to the worship of Allah.

Because of its public nature, Muslims believe it is inappropriate for a woman to practise itikaf in the mosque, but she is given the same spiritual reward if she withdraws to the place where she normally prays in her home.

Zakat-ul-fitr

The beginning of the next month is a time of celebration. After Id prayers, the day is spent in visits to friends and excursions. It is a time of special celebration for children, with gifts of money and new clothes. Each head of household donates a sum of money to the poor on behalf of each of his dependents. This is called **Zakat-ul-fitr**, and the celebration is known as Id-ul-fitr.

Zakah and sadaqah

The fourth pillar of Islam is the payment of zakah to the poor. Zakah should be given by every member of the community who has more than is considered necessary for them.

The giving of additional charity in the form of sadaqah is strongly recommended by Islam. Asmah narrated that the Prophet Muhammad (PBUH) said:

> '**Do not shut your purse; otherwise Allah too will withhold his blessings from you. Spend (in Allah's cause) as much as you can afford.**'
>
> Hadith Bukhari

Human beings are greedy and try to get as much as they can for themselves. Muslims believe that money and possessions are only loans from Allah. Some people are made wealthier than others as a way of testing their behaviour, but wealth is a burden to be avoided. As the Prophet Muhammad (PBUH) lay dying, he ordered that his few gold coins be distributed among the poor, as he did not want to meet his Lord with them in his possession.

While many Muslims are content to pay the zakah and give some additional money to charity, others seek to live in relative poverty, afraid that wealth will draw them away from their worship of Allah.

Tasks

1   Write a letter from a Muslim of your own age to a non-Muslim friend describing how your feelings have changed during the month of Ramadan. Include the anticipation, the anxiety, the joys of fasting and breaking the fast and the preparations for Id. Conclude by explaining how you have changed.

2   In small groups discuss the benefits to poor people of a system in which the rich have to give some of their wealth to the poor.

3   Muslims have to give $2\frac{1}{2}$ per cent of their savings above £500 as zakah. Work out how much should be given if they have £900 in the bank.

38

The pilgrimage to Makkah

The journey of a lifetime

Just as many people save for a special occasion or a holiday, Muslims save so that they can visit the holy sites around Makkah. This journey is the fifth pillar of the faith, the hajj.

The most important journey anybody makes is when they die. Many Muslims try to regard their pilgrimage as a rehearsal for that last journey. As pilgrims make preparations for their families during their absence, they remember that their next journey will not have a return ticket. The goodbyes between pilgrims and their families are hopeful, but a reminder that families will be separated by death and only sincere belief in Allah will bring reunion.

The first sight of the Ka'bah is a moment never forgotten

Ihram

Most people spend their lives concentrating on practical matters. It is important for pilgrims to leave their worries behind them. They are helped do do this by assuming the condition of ihram, which involves some restrictions. The most obvious sign of a pilgrim's status are the special clothes. Women pilgrims may wear any simple modest clothing, providing it reveals only their faces. Man wear two white garments to eliminate all differences in wealth and nationality. The king looks the same as the poor man. This closeness that lies at the heart of the pilgrimage is described by the Qur'an:

> **'Verily, this Brotherhood**
> **Of yours is a single Brotherhood,**
> **And I am your Lord**
> **And Cherisher: therefore**
> **Serve Me (and no other).'**
>
> Qur'an 21:92

By wearing ihram pilgrims appear before Allah as equal as they were on the day that they were born, and as they will do when they wear the simple white garments of the grave.

The Sacred Mosque

Every Muslim remembers their first sight of the **Ka'bah**, the first house built for the worship of Allah, which has for so long been the centre of their prayers. During the pilgrimage season the mosque is crowded with pilgrims from all nations. Their voices can be heard in supplication and prayer. Every pilgrim worships Allah with great intensity and humility.

During the initial visit to the Sacred Mosque, each pilgrim circles the Ka'bah. This rite, called **tawaf**, is full of memories of the prophets who trod this path before – Ibrahim and his son Isma'il, Muhammad and perhaps even Adam (PBUT). Pilgrims pray near the place where Ibrahim prayed, and they drink from the well of **Zamzam** as Isma'il drank.

Arafat

Standing on the plain of Arafat, on the ninth day of **Dhul-Hijjah** (the month of hajj), distinguishes the hajj from a mere visit. This is when all pilgrims feel their unity before Allah. Despite differences in language and custom,

The 'stand' at Arafat is the most important part of hajj

nationality and race, they are united in their worship of Allah. It is a day spent in intense supplication. In response to the requests of the pilgrims many sins are forgiven.

Aishah narrated that the Prophet Muhammad (PBUH) said:

> **'There is no other day on which Allah frees a larger number of his slaves from the fire of hell than the day of Arafat.'**

Hadith Muslim

This day spent at Arafat is a time when people of all nations meet each other on an equal basis, and can appreciate the meaning of the Qur'anic statement that they are 'one nation'.

The farewell

During the next two to three days, pilgrims complete the rest of the rites of hajj. These are ancient, some dating back to the time of Ibrahim and recalling the purity of his worship of Allah.

After completing hajj, many pilgrims stay in Makkah for a few days of private prayer. They may also visit Madinah, the town which welcomed the Prophet Muhammad (PBUH) and where he is buried. For many, Madinah is an oasis of peace and tranquillity. As pilgrims say their farewells, they hope fervently to return to the cradle of Islam, just one more time.

A first visit to the Ka'bah

One pilgrim remembers her first visit to the Holy Mosque in Makkah:

> 'The approach to the Holy Mosque from Jeddah is over a small hill. You are busy searching for the first sight of the mosque in the distance when suddenly there it is before you. As we drove past I saw the Ka'bah briefly through the wide doors. It was a sight that will remain with me for ever. The mosque was beautiful, but the Ka'bah seemed to shine, as though lit from within. It is the most wonderful feeling to pray there. The Ka'bah is before you as you pray, and all over the world there are people praying with you. They are behind you, but as well there are the people before you; after all this was the place where the prophets Ibrahim and Muhammad (PBUT) used to pray. It is like no other place on earth: you are totally surrounded by others praying with you, all worshipping the one god, Allah.'

Tasks

1   Select one of the places of religious significance around Makkah which has great meaning to a Muslim and describe its importance.

2   In small groups discuss how you felt when you spent your first night away from home. What did you say to your parents as you left? What else would you have done or said if you had thought you wouldn't be coming back?

3   Make a list of the ways in which someone's wealth or position is shown by their clothes. Why is this so difficult when a pilgrim is wearing ihram?

39

The final journey

Death

Death is the final journey. It is the journey from which there is no return, and which cannot be avoided. But Muslims believe that there will be a life to follow this life. If Allah was able to create every human being out of nothing then he will be able to do it again. Just as a vivid dream fades on waking, so our life on this earth will seem equally distant in the life to come. The hereafter (**akhirah**) is the true life, and our present experiences are only an introduction.

Muslims believe that human beings were created in order to worship their creator, to believe in him and to follow his injunctions concerning good and evil. Most Muslims will leave this life before the Last Day, when all life will end. As Muslims approach death they

Life on Earth comes to an end

endeavour to utter the shahadah. So just as this was the first sound they heard, it is the last sound that they make.

Burial

As death is inevitable, the family and friends of the deceased must accept that a life is over. While it may be a time of sadness, it should also be a period of spiritual renewal. Islam encourages the speedy burial of the body, with a simple ceremony. It is an opportunity for the community to gather round the family of the deceased, offering support and sympathy.

There are hadith that describe how the occupants of the grave will be aware of what is happening and, as the mourners depart, how they will be questioned in the grave by angels. Depending on their responses, they will wait either in comfort or in torment until the Day of Judgement.

The Last Day

Life on earth will eventually come to an end. Muslims believe that this will come about with such great upheaval and disaster that the inhabitants of the earth will wish that they were already safely in their graves. The Qur'an contains many such descriptions, mostly found in the shorter surahs, revealed before the Prophet's migration from Makkah to Madinah:

> 'When the sky is
> Torn apart,
>
> And listens to its Lord –
> And it must –
>
> And when the Earth
> Is flattened out,
>
> And throws up
> What is within it
> And becomes empty,
>
> And listens to its Lord –
> And it must –

Belief in Allah determines one's final resting place

then will come
Home the full Reality.

O human being!
Truly you are ever
Toiling on towards your Lord –
Painfully toiling, but you
Shall meet him.'

Qur'an 84:1–6

In English the poetic majesty of the original Arabic is lost, but such is its power that it still inspires awe and fear. Imagine the great strength needed to tear the sky above us to pieces. No one can know when the end will come, although there are many hadith that describe the circumstances that will exist just before it. On the Last Day Muslims believe that those who have died will be brought to life again, ready to be judged.

Heaven and hell

The purpose of a Muslim's life is to please Allah by acknowledging him as the creator; the final fate of all individuals depends on their behaviour. In the hereafter every sin will be punished in hell and every good deed rewarded in heaven. This is why Muslims have prayed and fasted, have saved for hajj and given in charity. Each and every one of these actions will have its reward. The other spiritual disciplines observed by the believer will also be rewarded: patience in adversity; repentance for slights and omissions; chastity in the face of temptation; truthfulness when confronted with lies; piety (taqwa) when surrounded with godlessness, and absolute dependence on Allah (tawakkul) through every up and down of life. It is the belief in Allah that will determine everyone's eternal abode. Muslims believe that the Qur'an has been sent as a guide to aid human beings on their path through life. For those who have followed the straight path a reward is due. The choice between mercy or wrath lies in belief and piety.

Tasks

1   Imagine you have entered the next life (either heaven or hell). Describe how you feel about the life you have left behind.

2   In small groups discuss what difference it would make to the way you feel if you knew that someone who hurt you would eventually be punished. Would this belief make you less likely to try to punish them yourself?

40

Holiness in words – the Torah

'… therefore, O Lord our God, when we lie down and when we rise up we will speak of your commandments and rejoice in the words of your Torah … for they are our life and the length of our days and we will meditate on them day and night.'

Prayer book

The Torah

Torah means 'instruction'. It is the name of the Jews' holy book. It contains the commandments God wants them to keep, as well as his guidance for moral living. This is why Jews have always regarded it as their most precious possession – it tells them how God wants them to conduct their lives. The Torah also tells Jews about their first ancestors and how they kept their faith in God, both in good times and in difficult ones. This is important, as it gives Jews a sense of identity.

Strictly speaking, 'Torah' refers to the teachings God revealed to the Jewish people at Mount Sinai. These are written in Hebrew and are known as the **Five Books of Moses.** In the synagogue, parchment scrolls of the Torah are kept in an honoured place called the ark. They are taken out and read to the congregation on certain days of the week, especially on Sabbaths and festivals. Whenever the scrolls are carried to and from the ark, the whole congregation rises to show respect for God's words.

However, Jews regard studying the Torah as more important than hearing it read. They study it in order to know how to fulfil God's commandments and to learn Jewish values. This is why Jews also use the word 'Torah' ('instruction') to include the whole of the **Tenakh,** the Jewish Bible. They often use it to mean the Talmud and later rabbinic writings, too, since these all show how the teachings revealed at Mount Sinai are to be understood.

But this is only one reason for studying the Torah. For Jews there is also the **mitzvah** (commandment) of engaging with the Torah itself, as a way of connecting with God. Jews believe that this is the most direct way of finding God.

A rabbi tells stories from the Torah – for Jewish children this is often the first step towards learning about their heritage

> 'The study of Torah is not a matter of learning "about" Judaism ... it establishes a connection between the learner and the source of the text.'
>
> Adin Steinsaltz

God's presence in the Torah

When we read any book, something of the author's personality comes across to us. This happens with the Torah, too. Indeed, Jews believe that God designed the Torah for this very purpose:

> '**I have written myself into the Torah and have given myself to you.**'
>
> Talmud

Jews take this to mean that the Torah is God's medium for communicating his will and wisdom to human beings. He does this through the Torah's stories, laws and ethical teachings. Even where the Torah deals with seemingly ordinary matters – someone's animal causing damage, the payment of labourers, or conversations between people – Jews see these as the physical expressions of lofty ethical and spiritual ideals. It is God transmitting his will through commandments and narratives to which we can relate. This is what the Talmud means when it says: 'The Torah speaks in the language of human beings'.

The Zohar explains this idea more fully:

> '**The stories of the Torah are its outer garments; woe to anyone who, looking at that garment, thinks it is the Torah itself ... a person's garments are plainly visible, but the pride of the garments is the person's body, and the pride of the body is the soul. Similarly the Torah has a body comprising its commandments and that body is wrapped around in garments of stories. Stupid people see only the garment; those who are a little wiser penetrate to the body; but the really wise see right through to the soul ... to the real Torah.**'

The words of the Torah are ordinary Hebrew words. Like any other words, they convey ideas and feelings. Yet, for Jews, they contain limitless depths. When Jews study the Torah, their minds are engaging with layers upon layers of meaning without end, for within is the infinite will of God himself.

This is why Jews call Torah study osek baTorah, 'occupying oneself with the Torah' – not just an exercise of the mind, but a total experience of God's presence.

Tasks

1 What would you expect to find in the Torah? What do you think is meant by the Torah giving Jews a sense of identity?

2 Why do Jews regard Torah study as important? Why do they call it osek baTorah?

3 The following extracts are from Ethics of the Fathers, written nearly 2,000 years ago. How do they help to explain what Torah study means to Jews?

'**Do not say I will study when I have free time, perhaps you will never have free time**' (2:5).

'**Minimize your business activities and occupy yourself with the Torah**' (4:12).

'**If you have learned much Torah, do not think of it as a great accomplishment. This is what you were created for**' (2:9).

'**It is beautiful to study Torah and have an occupation ... for all Torah study without work must in the end achieve nothing**' (2:2).

4 The children in the photo are taking their first steps towards Torah study. As a class, or in groups, discuss to what extent you think such preparation is necessary for experiencing the world of the spirit.

41

Holiness in space – Jerusalem and the Temple

'Let it be your will O Lord our God and God of our ancestors that you will have compassion on us and on your Temple and rebuild it very soon ...'

Prayer book

In the last unit we saw how Jews believe that God created the world and continuously sustains it. Jews understand this to mean that everything in nature is put there by God, that God is all around them and, in a way unknown to us, inside them. God's presence in all things makes the whole world holy.

At the same time, Jews regard Israel as especially holy: it is 'a land which the Lord your God cares for, and the eyes of the Lord your God are on it continuously, from the beginning till the end of the year' (Deuteronomy 11:12). Within Israel, Jerusalem is special: it is the Jews' 'Holy City' and they always turn to face it when they pray. Holier still is that part of Jerusalem where the Temple once stood.

The spiritual centre of the world

The site where the Temple stood has ancient associations reaching back to the very origins of the Jewish people. According to Jewish tradition, that is where Abraham prepared to sacrifice his son, Isaac, in obedience to God's command; there God blessed Jacob. For Jews, it is also bound up with the ultimate spiritual destiny of the world – it is the place where, one day, all humanity will worship God in harmony. Jews were expected to attend the Temple to celebrate the major festivals, and whole families would go together. For Jews, the site where it stood was, and still is, the holiest spot on earth.

The central part of the Temple was the 'Holy Place', where only priests were allowed to enter and, inside it, the 'Holy of Holies'. There,

no – one entered except the High Priest and only on **Yom Kippur**, the holiest day of the Jewish year. It housed the ark, the golden and wooden box made at God's command, upon which stood two cherubim, angel-like figures of gold, whose wings curved towards each other but did not touch. That empty space between their wing tips was the focal point of the Temple and, for Jewish people, of the entire world. There, God had told Moses: '... I will speak with you ... from between the two cherubim' (Exodus 25:22). In the **kabbalah**, the Jewish mystical tradition, that empty space is called 'the umbilical cord of the world', the point at which heaven and earth meet and a different dimension of reality breaks through into our universe.

The Temple site regained

Today, all that remains of the Jews' holiest site is the Western Wall, the outer wall of the second Temple that replaced the original one built by King Solomon. When the State of Israel was established in 1948, the Temple site was under Jordanian control. For nineteen years, no Jew was allowed to pray there.

On the morning of 7 July 1967, during the Six Day War, Jews regained their most sacred site. One writer described the scene as follows:

'Soon the esplanade was filled with paratroopers. The brigade commander signalled GHQ: "The Temple Mount is ours. Repeat: The Temple Mount is ours". ... Another paratroop unit made straight for the Western Wall ... The first soldier through gave a great shout: "The Western Wall! I can see the Wall", and then the rest rushed through to touch and kiss the hallowed stones. Tough paratroopers, who had fought hard and non-stop for 32

Festival prayers by the Western Wall

► hours, wept at the Temple wall over which their people had wailed for so many centuries …'

Janette Moore was a student in Jerusalem at the time. She relates how, on the following day, she: '… joined the heaving throng of over 200,000 Jews from all over Israel that made its way along that narrow road towards the Dung Gate … We were like a people dazed … Was this really happening? … We reached the gate and walked slowly through into the southern part of the Old City. Behind us was the ancient city of David; in front of us the remains of the Temple.'

Eventually, she reached the Wall itself, which: '… dominated the whole square; a huge majestic structure dwarfing the thousands of people at its foot … Gradually I inched my way forward. I stretched out my arm, fingers extended. At last I could touch the sacred stones with my fingertips. A little more effort and my cheek and my lips made contact, the tears running freely from my eyes. I was home.'

The Western Wall today

Since 1967, there have been daily services in front of the Wall. There are often several taking place at the same time in different parts of the concourse. Jews from all over the world feel a sense of personal pilgrimage when they travel there, some to join in the services, others for personal prayer or silent meditation.

The photo shows the scene in front of the wall during one of the major festivals. The men standing nearest the wall are priests. They are facing the congregation and pronouncing the traditional blessing of peace (see Tasks).

The Western Wall has a mystique uniquely its own. Even Jews who do not pray there regularly find themselves drawn to it.

'Twenty years have passed since last I visited the Western Wall with my father. Now I come with my five-year-old daughter on my shoulder. Why have I brought her here? Why did my father, who was not even religious, bother to bring me to the Western Wall when I was a child? Because … it saw the Temple in all its glory, it was a witness to its destruction, our destruction … and because it also symbolizes the future, and the hope. For the day will come when all Jews will gather here, the Temple will be rebuilt, and the Kingdom of David will be restored.'

Tasks

1   Which part of the Temple was the most sacred? What was it that made it holy? What might it mean to speak of the Temple site as holy today?

2   What is a 'sense of personal pilgrimage'? How might it differ from the obligatory pilgrimages of Biblical times?

3   David Shimoni (1886–1956), a Russian Jewish poet, once wrote: 'Through the deserts of diaspora you followed us, O Jerusalem … on every gallows you accompanied us, and our foremost blessing was always "Next year in Jerusalem"'. What do you think he was trying to express?

4   The blessing the priests in the photo are pronouncing is: 'May God bless you and protect you; May God make His face shine upon you and be gracious to you; May God turn His face to you and give you peace' (Numbers 6:22–7). Why do you think Jews regard this as important?

'Remember to keep the Sabbath day holy ... on it you must not do any kind of work ... for in six days the Lord made heaven and earth, the sea, and everything that is in them and rested on the seventh day; therefore the Lord blessed the sabbath day and made it holy.'

Exodus 20:8–11

The Sabbath is the holiest day of the week for Jewish people. They call it Shabbat or Shabbos, which means 'rest'. It lasts from sunset on Friday till the stars appear on Saturday night. Throughout this period, Jews are not permitted to do any melachah. This is often translated as 'work', but really it refers to certain types of creative task such as lighting a fire, baking, writing and sewing. On the Sabbath Jews are expected to put all their weekday affairs aside and turn their attention to prayer, Torah study and strengthening their family ties.

'The essence of Shabbat is to free oneself from the negative, narrow values of materialism ... to divert our creativity from the physical sphere to the realm of the spirit.'

Rabbi Eliyahu Dessler (1892–1953)

Preparing for Shabbat

Friday afternoon is a busy time in a Jewish home as cooking, vacuuming the floor, polishing shoes and many other tasks must all be done before Shabbat begins. One Jewish housewife writes:

'The top priorities, the "musts" of Shabbat preparation, are in most cases determined by the requirements of halachah (Jewish Law). For example, your cooking must be completed, your make-up applied and your appliances switched off by candle-lighting time ... in addition, you will have your personal priorities to consider, such as reading over the parashah (Torah reading for that week) or phoning your family to ►

► wish them "good Shabbos" before candle-lighting. Time must be budgeted for these activities, too.'

Just before sunset, women usher the Shabbat into their homes by lighting candles.

A foretaste of the world to come

With the lighting of the candles, a new atmosphere takes over. Only moments earlier, the house was a scene of frenetic activity as people hurried to beat the Shabbat deadline. Suddenly, it all stops:

'You now stand still. The pulse of life beats calmer. You recover your senses, relax from the yoke of your toil ... The Sabbath silently enters your soul and your home is transformed.'

Rabbi Samson Raphael Hirsch (1808–88)

But the new mood is not a just a feeling of unwinding after a spell of hard work. It is more a sense of having entered a different time frame. All around, the rest of the world moves on; cars and buses go by in the street, people are out shopping, telephones and fax machines carry messages back and forth across the planet – they are still tuned in to ordinary time. But for 25 hours, Jews will not be part of it. They have moved to an island where time and activity have no meaning other than for prayer, Torah study, rest and family togetherness. The Sabbath is outside ordinary time; it is, as the Talmud puts it, 'a taste of the world to come'.

Shabbat as a family event

Look at the family in the photo. They have returned from Friday night prayers in the synagogue and are sitting down to their Shabbat meal. This is one of a Jew's most precious moments. The room will have been prepared as for an honoured guest with the best tableware

The Shabbat meal is a time of family togetherness

laid out, because Jews think of the Shabbat as a queen who comes to visit each week. Most important of all, they are together as a family.

But this is nothing like a birthday party or a similar family gathering. The telephone does not ring, the TV remains silent, no one is going anywhere. It is a relaxed, unhurried meal. Between courses they sing songs praising God and the beauty of the Shabbat and tell stories about the great men and women of Jewish history.

One young man, a busy doctor working in a South African hospital, had never experienced any of this until he was invited to spend Shabbat with a religious family. He writes:

'The first thing that struck me on Shabbat in that home was that no one was going anywhere. The familiar rush of each member of the family to his own activities was absent, everyone was together and simply enjoying being there.'

Like many secular Jews, he had been brought up to think of Shabbat as a day of burdensome restrictions. But as he spent Shabbat after Shabbat with that family, he began to discover that:

'The weekdays are spent building, developing, constantly moving towards a goal, whereas Shabbat is itself something of that ultimate and absolute goal … On Shabbat the individual and the family are not going anywhere; they have arrived. ►

► The experience is … the indescribable feeling … of permanence within change.'

The afterglow of Shabbat

When the stars appear on Saturday night, Shabbat is over. After evening prayers, the family gathers for **havdalah,** a short ceremony marking the departure of the Shabbat. Then they start washing the dishes, vacuuming, opening their letters. They have returned to the ordinary, busy world of work. But for the rest of Saturday evening something of the Shabbat atmosphere remains. In some communities, people come together to 'see the Shabbat on its way' with a small party known as melaveh demalka (accompanying the Shabbat).

Here is part of a children's song. It expresses how Jews feel about coming to the end of their special day.

'Shabbos is going away,
The sky's getting dark, it's the end of the day,
O Shabbos you really should know,
We're sorry to see you go.
But you will come back next week we know,
You will come back for we love you so,
Give thanks to Hashem (God),
Who will bring Shabbos back again.'

Tasks

1 Why is Shabbat important for Jews? How do Jews emphasise its importance (a) before it begins (b) after it has ended? Why would doing a melachah be inconsistent with keeping Shabbat as a holy day?

2 What do you think is meant by 'to divert our creativity from the physical sphere to the realm of the spirit' and 'on Shabbat, the individual and family are not going anywhere; they have arrived'?

3 What does the children's song tell you about the way Jews think of Shabbat?

43 Holiness in good deeds – the image of God

'Who is worthy of being called human? Only someone who performs good deeds'.

Midrash

Most people would agree that we should behave morally, although it is not always easy to give reasons why. Just having a strong sense of justice or compassion may not always be sufficient. After all, how might we behave on days when we simply did not happen to feel compassionate?

For Jews, the real basis of moral behaviour is the belief that each human being is created Godlike.

'Then God said: "Let us make a human in our image" ... So God created the human in his image, in the image of God he created ... male and female.'

Genesis 1:26–7

The image of God

The idea of humans having been created in God's image means, as Rabbi Elie Munk (1900–78) put it, every person 'bears within them a spark of the divine spirit ... to this spark they owe the immortality of their souls and the light of understanding which shines within them, permitting them to know God, to love Him and cleave to Him'.

The implication of this is, in the words of one rabbi:

'Love of one's fellow human beings which is not motivated and nourished by the realization that they are created in God's image, is doomed to failure ... Without this realization, a person is merely a mass of bones, nerves, muscles, and blood that happens to function in an orderly fashion ... Only when we realize that humans ► alone are fashioned in the image of the creator of heaven and earth are they suddenly transformed from an inconsequential and insignificant being into one that is without parallel.'

At the root of this idea is the belief that each person is put on this Earth for a purpose. An ancient Jewish teaching has it that 'God desired a dwelling place among low creatures' **(Midrash)**. 'Low creatures' refers to human beings, i.e. beings who are largely unaware of God's presence and capable of denying that he exists.

We have no idea why God might want this. But what is important is the awareness that it is up to us to prepare the world by making it a purer, more spiritual place. Jews believe that people accomplish this when they live according to the seven Noachide Laws – not to worship anything other than God, not to blaspheme, neither to murder, steal, commit sexual perversions nor be cruel to animals, and to set up a system of justice. They see the Noachide Laws as the basic requirement for living a moral and spiritual life.

This means that Jews are taught to see each individual as a creature fashioned bodily, mentally and emotionally to be a partner with God – an 'image' of God.

The image of God in others

Recognizing other people as living 'images of God' means treating them with respect and consideration – even with love. Rabbi Samson Raphael Hirsch, commenting on the verse 'You shall love your neighbour as yourself' (Leviticus 19:18), wrote:

'… we are to rejoice in his good fortune, and grieve over his misfortune as if it were our own. We are to assist at everything that furthers his well-being and happiness as if we were working for ourselves, and must keep trouble away from him as assiduously as if it threatened ourselves … this love … is something that is expected from us towards all our fellow-men in the name of God.'

This is expressed most clearly in the Jewish attitude to the disadvantaged. Jews see them as living 'images of God' – people with the capacity to bring God's plan closer to fulfilment – who are suffering poverty, physical or mental handicap, a debilitating illness or domestic abuse. Providing help, comfort or simply a shoulder to cry on is not 'charity' – it is responding to the divinity within them.

The image of God in oneself

Good deeds also affect the doer, for 'God's image' also means the ability to act like God.

> '**What does it mean "You shall walk after the Lord your God" (Deuteronomy 13:5)? It means that you shall walk in his ways. Just as he clothes the naked, visits the sick and comforts mourners, so you must clothe the naked, visit the sick and comfort mourners.**'
>
> Talmud

Doing good refines the doer. But Judaism goes further – it teaches that good deeds are the route to holiness. Jews understand this to mean that when they try to relieve pain and poverty or bring joy and hope to others, they realize their own potential to be 'images of God'.

One Jewish thinker pointed out that 'It is not said: "You shall be full of awe for I am holy", but "You shall be holy, for I the Lord your God am holy"' (Leviticus 19:2).

'Images of God' in need

Tasks

1   How do Jews understand the verse 'God created the human in his image'? Why do they regard this verse as the foundation of morality?

2   Look at the photos. What areas of need do they portray? Think of ways in which ordinary people (i.e. not only professionals, like nurses) might help. What do Jews believe would be the benefit to (a) the recipient (b) the doer?

3   Explain what you think the writers quoted in this unit meant by 'bear within them a spark of the divine spirit'; 'This love … is expected from us towards all our fellow men in the name of God' and 'our own life as an image of his will'.

Holiness in marriage – family purity

'The Torah lists the sexual relationships forbidden to us and then tells us: "You shall be holy" (Leviticus 19:2). This teaches you that even in a permitted relationship you must conduct yourself with sanctity.'

Rabbi Moses ben Nachman (1194–1270)

Jews have always seen marriage as the framework in which two people can develop as human beings. In the Talmud and Zohar, an unmarried man and an unmarried woman are both called 'unfinished'. Marriage is the means by which they grow to see each other 'in the Jewish way; with respect, as partners in life and not just as means of procreation or mere sexual objects. Not that the erotic element is invalid, but that, from a Jewish point of view, it is not enough' (Adin Steinsaltz).

However, the Jewish ideal is, as the Midrash puts it: 'Neither a man living alone nor a woman living alone, nor the two of them together without God's presence'. Jews believe that people grow to full maturity when they develop their relationship in accordance with God's will – in effect, making God a third partner in their marriage. This is why they call marriage kiddushin: 'making holy'. It expresses the ideal of bringing holiness into every aspect of the relationship.

Sanctity in sexuality

The sexual union is the most intimate physical expression of the bond between two people. In Jewish thinking, it is also a bond with God. 'There are three partners involved in forming a child,' says the Talmud. 'Mother and father produce the body, God provides the soul.' A recent writer elaborates:

'One of the reasons sex is so holy is that it has the ability to accomplish something that is beyond the power of any other ▶ human function – namely, drawing a soul down to the world, and producing a living human being.'

Aryeh Kaplan

One woman who lectures widely on the position of women in Judaism writes:

'The idea that love is a holy affair is something intuitively understandable to a woman … She has been granted a natural ability to appreciate marital intimacy as holy and divine. Therefore, the merely physical is often not sufficient for her. In order to function as a total woman, she must feel that intimacy is more than a physical act. It must involve her soul and provide her with deep emotional fulfilment.'

Tehilla Abramov

Family purity

Central to the sanctity of Jewish marital relations is taharat hamishpachah – family purity. This is a rhythm alternating between times when a husband and wife may express their love physically and times when they may not. From the onset of her period, for a minimum of twelve days, all physical contact between her and her husband is strictly forbidden. They may only resume the physical side of their relationship after she returns from the **mikveh** – a pool of natural water (see below) where, under the eye of a female attendant, she immerses her entire body.

To an outsider, the idea of having no physical contact for 40 per cent of each month may seem like a sure way to destroy a marriage. In fact, the reverse is true. Rabbi Aryeh Kaplan points out that:

'… according to most marriage counsellors, a significant reason for married couples drifting apart is that they simply become bored with each other … A common response is for one or both partners to seek sexual liaisons with individuals other than their spouse … The monthly separation tends to renew the sexual relationship and thus stabilizes the marriage bond.'

It also creates opportunities for husband and wife 'to strengthen the more subtle aspects of the relationship. Both partners can become more aware of the advantages of speaking together, friendship, and non erotic closeness' (Adin Steinsaltz). But taharat hamishpachah is more than a device for maintaining a couple's interest in one another. At its core is the belief that human sexuality is holy and, as such, is to be approached with reverence.

The mikveh

The photo below shows a 2,000-year-old mikveh – the oldest yet discovered. It was built at Masada, a hill-top fortress near the Dead Sea where, after the destruction of Jerusalem in 70 CE, about a thousand Jews – men, women and children – made their last stand against the Romans. Yet, even under siege, they found it unthinkable to be without a mikveh to maintain the sanctity of their married life.

The photo above shows a present-day mikveh. It shows modern materials and architectural design brought together to create an attractive, pleasant atmosphere. Atmosphere is important, for:

A modern mikveh

'From an emotional perspective, the woman must be totally submerged in the experience of mikveh. She must appreciate it as a holy process, granting her new sensitivity to spirituality. The sense of purity, the anticipated reunion with her husband and, most importantly, the satisfaction of fulfilling God's will, all combine to create an uplifting experience.'

Tehilla Abramov

Tasks

1 Why do Jews see marriage as important? What steps do they take to preserve holiness in marital relations?

2 Summarize the first extract from Tehilla Abramov's book in your own words. What do you think she means when she writes of 'marital intimacy as holy and divine'?

3 Popular magazines often print articles about people's sexual experiences. As a class or in groups, discuss to what extent you think such articles influence people's attitudes? Do you think they encourage young people to see each other primarily as sexual objects and, if so, should we welcome that or should we try to change it? Remember to include the Jewish attitude in your debate.

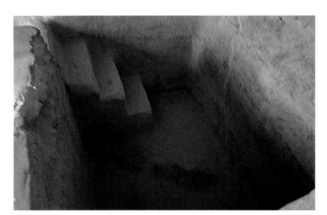
The Masada mikveh, 1st century CE

45 Holiness in death – bereavement and beyond

'Blessed are you O Lord our God, King of the world, the true judge.'

Blessing said by mourners

Judaism is a life-affirming religion. It teaches that preserving life takes precedence over almost all of the commandments.

Nonetheless, death comes to everyone. And even when it is expected – say, an elderly person at the end of a long illness – it rarely fails to affect those close to the deceased. One writer describes 'a rage of conflicting emotions … bewilderment and paralysis, agony and numbness, guilt and anger, fear and futility and pain – and also release from care and worry'.

At such a time, it is often difficult to experience spirituality in the usually understood sense of something beautiful and desirable.

Confronting God

However, a bereaved person often does feel the presence of God, if only in an oppressive, even unbearable way. They might feel angry with God; they might feel that he is unjust or that he is punishing them. Even non-believers have been known to blame God at a time of intense grief.

In a curious way, these negative emotions express a deeply rooted awareness that God is intervening in people's lives. Even those who scream out against God in utter fury are, at that very moment, confronting him. At the very least, bereavement often makes people turn to God and ask 'why?'

Yitzchak Vorst is a Dutch rabbi. When his three-year-old son, Boruch, was killed by a car, he wrote:

'I believe in God. And that is precisely why now, in my almost unbearable grief, I ask ►

how a loving God could allow such a dreadful, terrible thing to happen – to wrench from me a child who was part of my heart. If I did not believe in God, I would not be surprised that there is so much suffering in the world. But I do believe in God. And for this reason I grope and seek an answer.'

Sometimes people experience sublime emotions in the midst of grief. Reuben Avinoam, an American–Jewish poet, had a son who was killed fighting in Israel's War of Independence in 1948. At the end of the **shiva**, the week of mourning, Avinoam wrote:

'Incline thine ear, O God,
Consider a brief space
In this night hour of sombre rage
The word of parents bewildered by bereavement.
We approach thee not with regret, nor complaint.
Nor do we come to litigate with thee,
Only thanks pouring from the wound of our heart we offer thee.
Accept it, O God … thanksgiving be to thee: For pleasant years,
For one and twenty years
Wherein thou didst honour us with him and lent him us.'

Life beyond death

Rabbi Vorst writes of the people who came to visit him and his wife during their shiva. One visitor's presence was particularly traumatic:

'The woman who drove the car which hit our child also comes to see us – with a friend who had been with her in the automobile … The other visitors, realizing ►

► who she is, fall silent. It is as if they regard her as an enemy, as the murderess of our child. But we try to put her at ease and tell her that we do not blame her, for everything is foreseen and arranged by God. Even if she had not driven too fast, Boruch would not have been with us any more. For his time had evidently come.'

These words, point to an acute awareness of the relationship between this life and the world of the spirit. The Jewish view of life and death can perhaps best be understood by comparing it to a stage with the actors waiting in the wings to go on. As each one goes on stage, they are given basic guidelines so that they know why they are there and what is expected. For the rest of the time, they try to carry out their task while interacting with the other players and getting caught up with other things. At unexpected times each one will be called off the stage to be assessed, after which they will move on to something new.

Similarly, Jews think of the period before birth, life on this Earth and existence after leaving it as successive phases in a soul's career. In Jewish terms, we do not really belong here. Our true home is elsewhere; we are simply put on this Earth to play our part in furthering God's plan. However long or short our stay may be, as soon as we have had sufficient time and opportunities to complete that which we came for, we are taken back to where we belong.

Put in this way, however painful bereavement might be, it is ultimately comforting to those who remain to realize that their loved one has not 'died' in any final sense but has moved on to the next stage of life. This is why, in some Jewish communities, a Yarzheit (anniversary of a person's death) is marked by a small celebration. They are not recalling the departed person's time on earth but celebrating their present state in another dimension of reality.

Graves as holy sites

Apart from the loss of relatives, Jews experience another kind of bereavement – the loss of a

Prayers at a graveside

teacher. We saw on pages 82–3 how studying the Torah is an important way in which Jews connect with God. For this reason, those who teach the Torah are held in great esteem.

The photo shows Jews praying at the graveside of a great teacher in northern Israel. They are not praying to the teacher, nor trying to contact his spirit. Such things are strictly forbidden to Jews. But through association with the person buried there, they can feel more tuned in to God's presence than in other places.

Tasks

1 What emotions might a bereaved person experience? How might something of spiritual value emerge from them?

2 What do you think Rabbi Vorst meant when he wrote: 'I grope and seek an answer'?

3 Summarize the extract from Reuben Avinoam's poem in your own words. What does it tell you about his relationship with God?

4 How might the Jewish view of life and death help a person come to terms with bereavement?

5 Look at the Jews in the photo. Why are they praying by a graveside? (You may want to refer to pages 94–5 here.)

46 Holiness in life's journey – teshuva

'The gates of prayer are sometimes open and sometimes closed; but the gates of repentance are always open.'

Midrash

When Jews speak of repentance they use the word teshuva – 'returning'. They believe that, deep down, everyone is connected with God. Sin can obstruct that connection – 'your sins separate you from your God' (Isaiah 59:2) – but never destroy it. The link with God can be re-established through teshuva, which Adin Steinsaltz defined as 'a spiritual reawakening, a desire to strengthen the connection between oneself and the sacred'.

Springboards to teshuva

The desire to do teshuva can arise in a various ways. The Talmud tells the story of Eliezer ben Durdai, a well-known sinner. One day, a prostitute he was with made a joke about him being lost for ever and never finding his way back to God. In a sudden, overwhelming realization that this was true, he left her and wandered out to the hills where he started to think about the direction his life had taken. Tears came to his eyes and he began to pray for forgiveness. So sincere and intense was his teshuva that his soul left him and he was taken straight into heaven.

People may also be moved to teshuva when they feel that their lives lacks meaning or direction. Many Jews today are brought up, as one writer describes it, they are:

'no longer certain just what makes them a people…they see themselves as anything but holy, they interpret in a negative way the things that make them Jewish and different from others … A group once sure of itself and convinced of its value seems to have forgotten why it has come into being. Everyday reality…has become a long ▶

▶ succession of meaningless but uncongenial encounters.'

Sometimes people do feel an emptiness in their lives. They start searching for meaning; they might try to create their own meaning – though this often fails to satisfy because they really want something deeper. That is often when they start thinking about a relationship with God.

Not only those who feel remote from God may be aroused to teshuva. Deeply religious Jews who pray three times a day, observe the Shabbat and live moral lives sometimes feel a desire to do more. One writer described it like this:

'This movement of the soul toward renewed connectedness can also come about in one who has never sinned, yet who feels called upon to draw closer to holiness.'

The awakening from above

So far, we have looked at situations where the desire for teshuva comes from the individual. The Zohar calls this 'the awakening from below'. There is also an 'awakening from above', i.e. when God acts, as Rabbi Schneur Zalman of Liadi (1745–1813) puts it, 'to arouse a person from their slumber in the emptiness of this world … as we see, there are people who feel a sudden urge to pray … without knowing how this feeling came to them'.

This idea of an 'awakening from above' is rooted in the Jewish belief that God wants people to have a relationship with him and constantly creates opportunities for them to recognize his presence. He might shower them with blessings so that they will be moved to thank him; he might bring hardship so that they will seek his help. God may manoeuvre people to make a journey, change jobs or do something impulsive, just to bring them to where they can encounter him. Jews believe that he never coerces but gives each man and woman the choice to either recognize or ignore the divine promptings in the things that happen in their lives.

Obstacles to teshuva

Teshuva often means overcoming obstacles within oneself. One major difficulty is people's resistance to acknowledging their own faults – what one 19th-century rabbi attributed to 'the self love that justifies all wrongdoings'. Another is a mistaken apprehension about what they might be undertaking – as a present-day rabbi explained: 'Many who are not Torah observant, but who have a desire to become so, are frightened by the far-reaching changes in their lifestyles that will be needed … They believe that the life of an observant Jew is one of hardship and austerity'.

A more subtle obstacle is secularism – an attitude or frame of mind wherein people take it for granted that religion is irrelevant. Secularism is fairly recent. Until the 18th century, most people did believe in God in some form. During and after the 18th century, thinkers valued reason above everything else; anything that did not have a basis in reason was dismissed. This was the beginning of a process that, during the following century, encouraged people to try to explain the nature of the universe, the origin of living species and the workings of the human mind without reference to God. So God came to seem increasingly unreal. Today, many people are brought up with secular values and take them for granted.

This has steered us to look at the world in secular categories. We think of theft as a crime but not a sin; we take medicine when we are ill but do not pray; we can gaze at a spectacular sunset and admire its beauty but not see it as the work of God. Secularism has dulled our ability to look at the world and find divinity.

Anyone wanting to do teshuva must confront all these obstacles and be willing to challenge their own ways of thinking and functioning. But overcoming obstacles is only the

One of nature's wonders – see Task 4

beginning, because teshuva is not, as one writer puts it, 'inner tranquillity and peace of mind', but 'a continuous going, a going with God, a going to God, day after day, year after year'.

Tasks

1 What was it about the prosititute's remark that made Eliezer ben Durdai react in the way he did? The rabbis who compiled the Talmud only included stories that had some religious value. Why do you think they included this story?

2 One of the writers quoted in this unit spoke of life being 'a long succession of meaningless and uncongenial encounters'. Explain what this means. How might this feeling be a factor in people doing teshuva?

3 What is meant by 'the awakening from below' and 'the awakening from above'? How do Jews see these working in people's lives? Is it always possible to distinguish between them? Explain your answer.

4 Look at the photo above. How might the wonders of nature prompt people to think about God?

5 People are often ready to spot faults in others yet amazingly resistant to seeing the same faults in themselves. What do you think the rabbi quoted meant when he attributed this to 'self love'?

47

The inner journey – Sikh spirituality

There are two main types of people according to the Sikh faith: those who trust in themselves, and those who trust in God. They are called **manmukh** (a self-centred person) and **gurmukh** (a God-centred person). The spiritual way for a Sikh is to be God-centred, but people have a natural tendency towards the manmukh in us. Sikhs also believe that, while living, people inhabit two worlds. The first is the outer world, which is physical, and which we can experience through our senses: we can see, hear, smell, taste and touch it, and to us it is real. In the Sikh scriptures this world is described as 'illusion', or maya. The second world is the living presence of God, which we experience through leading a spiritual life of prayer and meditation (**Nam Simran**), and cultivating and nourishing our inner selves.

The manmukh condition

A manmukh is a person who lives for the self, working for personal satisfaction, gain and pleasure. A manmukh views the world as a way of fulfilling personal ambition, collecting wealth and property. The family, husband or wife and children also become part of the manmukh's personal property. Other beings only count as possessions, means of gaining status. Satisfying physical needs and greed are very important. A manmukh is basically selfish, does not care for others and feels no responsibility for anybody else. A manmukh follows his or her own wisdom and mind, and spends life in wrong or even evil pursuits. This is known as manmat. Sikhs believe that there are five broad types of wrong inclination:

- lust (kam)
- anger (karodh)
- greed (lobh)
- emotional attachment (moh)
- arrogance (ahunkar).

These stand in the way of following God's path. The person who follows them loses the way to the spiritual path. At the end of their human life, such people enter the cycle of transmigration into other life forms, and thereby lose the only opportunity to gain salvation.

Becoming gurmukh

Sikhs believe that human beings have within their bodies the ray of God's light. They also believe that the purpose or goal of human life is to merge with the supreme light of God – in the same way as one small candle near a large candle gets absorbed into its light. God is the original and ultimate source, from whom people become separated when they are born, and to whom they return at the end of life. Sikhs believe that we should remember that God is where we come from.

However, reaching God depends on how we lead our lives. Human birth is precious and is not obtained easily or frequently. It is like the fruit of a tree which falls off, never to be reattached to the branch. Therefore, every effort should be made to remember our origin and to keep the light within the body glowing. Humans are also charged by God to take care of this Earth, nature and other creatures and life-forms, and not to exploit them for our selfish desires. A gurmukh leads the life of gurmat (literally 'according to the Guru's wisdom'), a way of life which brings the presence of God into everyday life. A gurmukh acknowledges the presence of God by obeying the command 'Jap', which means 'repeating the name of God'. God is the source of life, and by doing the Jap, the inner self is opened to God. A gurmukh says 'yes' to God and 'yes' to spiritual life. Through leading the life of gurmat, gurmukhs fill their own lives and those around them with the name of God – like the fragrance of blossom filling the forest air. There are hundreds of passages that describe the lifestyle and attributes of a gurmukh. Here are two examples:

Amar Das, the gurmukh, serves his Guru by collecting water from the river for his bath

'There is peace within a gurmukh,
Imbued with the Name in body and mind:
Thinks of the Name, reads of the Name,
Concentrates on the Name,
Receives the wealth of the Name.
Stress goes away.
Meets the true Guru: the Name grows.
Desire and hunger all go away.
The Name is obtained.'

Guru Granth Sahib 1317

In this hymn the phrase 'the Name' stands for God.

'The gurmukh way is the true way,
Which gently roots in a disciple's home.
The gurmukh way is the true wealth,
Which gathers as dust on feet.
The Guru's follower's bathing
Is to receive Guru's wisdom
And to remove the filth of bad thoughts.
The worship of the true disciple
Is to respect and to love another.
The obedience of the Guru's disciple

Is to treasure the Guru's preaching
As a precious garland round the neck.
The living of a Guru's disciple
Is to live like the dead without pride
And to reflect on the Guru's word.'

Amrit Kirtan 638

Tasks

1 If you had a choice, would you choose to be a manmukh or a gurmukh? Why?

2 What do Sikhs believe happens to people when they die, if they have spent their lives in evil pursuits?

3 Discuss why someone might choose to remain manmukh.

4 Why do many people wish to become gurmukh?

48

Achieving the goal

Guru Granth Sahib, the Sikh holy book, shows that the way to achieve the goal is to lead a God-centred life. It is said in Guru Granth Sahib that anyone who leads a God-centred (gurmukh) life will appear radiant in God's presence, after death. They will achieve oneness with God and help others to achieve salvation. Sikhs believe that a gurmukh, a God-centred person, attains spiritual fulfilment by leading life in a way similar to that of the water lily. A water lily has its roots in the muddy water of the pond, receives its sustenance from it and has many branches and leaves, but it flowers up out of the muddy water. In the same way, a God-centred person performs duties properly but stays detached from the attachments of the world and constantly remembers that the purpose of life is to remember God and to pray.

Recitation of Japji Sahib in the morning at home

Living as a Sikh

Practising Sikhs lead a life of religious discipline at home and outside. They get up well before dawn and take a bath or shower. They put on clean clothes and then sit down cross-legged for meditation and morning prayer. The time before dawn has special spiritual significance. It has a special name – Amritvela – which means 'the time of the shower of spiritual nectar'. Sikhs believe that those who rise, cleanse themselves and pray have a wonderful opportunity to be soaked in calming peace and joy.

The spiritual definition of a Sikh

According to a passage in the Guru Granth Sahib, a Sikh is defined in this way:

> **'One who wants to be called a Sikh
> Should awake early morning,
> Be alert, before dawn, have a bath in the sacred pool (of Amritsar) of immortality,
> Sing the Guru's hymns at the day-break,
> Remember God while sitting and standing (doing daily work).'**

Guru Granth Sahib 305

Balanced life

Sikhs should lead spiritually balanced lives. This is attained through self-discipline, meditation, worship and moral and virtuous living. In this way one is at peace in oneself, one can feel the presence of God around and be in spiritual harmony with the environment. Sikhs describe this condition as **sahaj**, which means 'leading a life of spiritual and physical balance'. This is the way a person achieves liberation while still living. It is through God's grace that liberation is granted. A Sikh is blessed through God's grace and this may be unasked and freely bestowed by God on the believer. There is a beautiful verse in the Adi Granth about one way through which God may show grace:

'God stands alongside for the work of
his holy people;
God himself comes to work with them'.

Guru Granth Sahib 783

God is with us when we work to do good for
fellow beings and supports our spiritual actions.
Therefore it is our spiritual duty to develop love
for God. It is in this love that there is peace, and
countless blessings are achieved in life on Earth
and life hereafter. Here is how the fifth Guru
Arjan describes that experience of love of God:

'With the love of God eternal peace is attained.
With the love of God there is no suffering.
With the love of God the dirt of self-centredness
is removed.
With the love of God immaculate state is
achieved forever.
My friend, cultivate such love for God,
Who is the sustainer of every life and
every heart.
With the love of God all treasures are received.
With the love of God the pure name enters
the mind.
With the love of God fame is bestowed.
With the love of God stress and anxiety
are removed.
With the love of God the ocean of death
is crossed.
With the love of God the messenger of hell
stays away.
With love of God all are saved.
The love of God continues with the mortal
after death.
By self alone one neither finds God nor
forgets ego.
The one to whom God shows grace
Joins the congregation of the righteous.
Nanak says, "O God I am a sacrifice to you
As you are the shelter and strength of saints".'

Guru Granth Sahib 391

The love of God is the way which opens doors
to oneness with God. This love achieves
fulfilment through God's grace in life in the
world. We are provided with the things we
need: food, shelter and comforts for the body;
but we are also provided with food for the mind
and soul; peace, contentment, humility, love

and the company of the spiritually uplifted.
Furthermore, the fear of death is removed
and there is the excitement of union with
the divine. It is only through love that one
finds God.

Guru Nanak has decribed the link between life
on Earth and the life hereafter in the final verse
of Japji Sahib:

Air, the Guru, water the father,
Earth, the great mother,
Day and night, male and female nurses
In whose laps the whole world plays.
Good and bad deeds are presented in
divine court.
They determine who stays close to God
and who is distanced.
Those who have prayed,
Leave the world with righteous toil.
Nanak says, their faces are radiant
And many more are saved with them.

Guru Granth Sahib 8

Love of God, leading a spiritual and moral life,
doing good deeds and regualar prayer help a
person to achieve the ultimate goal of oneness
with God.

Tasks

1 Explain in your own words the
   idea of the water lily and how
   it describes gurmukh.

2 Is it possible to live the balanced life Sikhs
   are told to follow? Discuss your views.

3 Explain how and why Sikhs believe you
   may experience grace.

4 Why is love of God important to Sikhs?

49

Worship at home

Reading from Guru Granth Sahib in the prayer room at home

worship and towards the holy book, the Guru Granth Sahib, and it is also considered to be a preparation for spiritual experience.

Morning prayer – Japji Sahib

The main morning prayer is called Japji Sahib, and forms the first chapter of the Guru Granth Sahib. The first verse of the Japji Sahib is called the mool mantra, and describes the attributes of God. Children are encouraged to learn it by heart:

> **'One God (Ik Onkar)**
> **Truth is the Name (Sat Nam)**
> **Creator (Karta Purakh)**
> **Without fear (Nir Bhau)**
> **Without hatred (Nir Vair)**
> **Immortal (Akaal Murat)**
> **Is neither born nor dies (Ajooni Sai Bhang)**
> **Found through Guru's grace (Gur Parsaad)**
> **Recite (Jup)**
> **True in the beginning (Aad Sach)**
> **True in all ages (Jugaad Sach)**
> **True now. (Hai Bhi Sach)**
> **Nanak truth shall ever be. (Nanak Hosi Bhi Sach)**

Pahli Pauri (Japji Sahib, first verse)

In most Sikh homes there are framed pictures of Guru Nanak, the first Guru; Guru Gobind Singh, the tenth Guru, and Harmandir Sahib, 'the Temple of God', also known as the Golden Temple, where Guru Arjan installed the Adi Granth in 1604. These pictures are usually in a special place in the living room. There may also be some calendars depicting pictures of the gurus, alongside some family pictures.

In some Sikh homes (if space allows), a room may be kept as a prayer room. The central focus in it is the Sikh holy book, Guru Granth Sahib, which will be draped in fine, coloured materials. These coverings are called romallas. There may also be decorations and flowers in vases and some money offerings. As a mark of reverence, shoes are not allowed in the room and the head should be covered. This is a mark of respect shown at entering the place of

There are several morning prayers: Japji Sahib (written by Guru Nanak); Shabad Hazare (composed by Guru Nanak and Guru Arjan, the fifth guru), and Jap Sahib and ten verses called Swayyas (compositions of the tenth Guru, Gobind Singh). They are usually recited from a daily prayer book known as Gutka. All the daily prayers are taken from Guru Granth Sahib and the Dasam Granth, the holy book which includes the compositions of Guru Gobind Singh.

Nam Simran

Nam Simran literally means 'remembering and repeating the name of God'. Apart from the recitation of the daily prayers, it is important that some time is spent on meditation and repetition of the word 'Waheguru', which means 'Wonderful Lord'. (This is known as nam japna.) Sikh parents teach their very young children to sit still for a short time and repeat the word, as a way of introducing them to the faith as soon as they learn to speak. Teaching the first verse of Japji Sahib is usually the next step.

Silent recitation of the word helps people to relate to their inner selves and to concentrate on the divine. To help their concentration, some people use a mala (rosary). A mala may be made of steel, cotton or woollen beads. It usually contains 108 beads, but sometimes a small rosary of 27 beads (simrana) is used, as this is more practical to carry around for prayer. The value of nam japna, meditation on God, as the first essential principle of the Sikh faith, is described in many verses in the Guru Granth Sahib. For example, one hymn, the Sukhmani Sahib, says:

> 'Pray, pray pray,
> and obtain peace.'

Guru Granth Sahib 262

A mala, as an aid to nam japna

The meditational prayer helps people forget their worries about life, and experience inner peace. However, it should not be a simply mechanical repetition but a conscious activity, which touches our deep thoughts and transforms us. It means listening to our inner self, and being aware of our heartbeat. Guru Nanak says in Japji Sahib:

> 'By listening one gets truth,
> divine wisdom and contentment;
> By believing one realizes truth and faith.'

Guru Granth Sahib 3

Work and prayer

During the day, a Sikh is expected to work hard either at work or at home, or by doing voluntary service, and to be honest, truthful, just, caring and humble in dealings with others. Nam Simran can also be done during all these activities. A passage in Guru Granth Sahib tells us that: 'Liberation can be achieved while laughing, playing, changing and dining'. The only elation and excitement Sikhs wish for is that of the Name. 'May the glow of the Name be upon me day and night,' says Guru Nanak.

In the evening, Sikhs say Rahras, the evening prayer, and before going to bed they perform the final short prayer, Kirtan Sohila, and thank God for a fulfilling and safe day.

Tasks

1. Discuss why Sikhs are taught to pray before dawn.

2. Why is it important to pray at the end of the day?

3. Discuss how a mala might help concentration.

4. What is the purpose of meditation for a Sikh?

50 The Guru Granth Sahib and women of faith

The Guru Granth Sahib has a very special place for Sikhs in their spiritual, religious and community lives. For most Sikhs the book is a living guru, and no Sikh ceremony can take place outside its presence, whether naming a new baby, an engagement ceremony, a wedding or a funeral service. The Guru Granth Sahib is a source of great inspiration and a symbol of great respect for male and female Sikhs, both at a personal level and at the community level.

It is a matter of great inspiration to many Sikh women that their faith provides them with equal access to God through examples in the scriptures, through the Sikh principles and practice, and through the role of women in shaping Sikh history. Here is how one Sikh woman describes the importance of the Guru Sahib to her:

'Every time I open the Guru Granth Sahib I wonder at the beauty and simplicity of the hymns. My early memory of a hymn which I learnt from my grandfather is still as fresh today as the day when I learnt it as a young child. As my understanding has grown, I have found the words in the hymn a source of great inspiration in my daily life of stresses and strains.'

Here is her translation of this hymn:

'Awake in peace,
Stay in peace;
There is no fear
with such understanding.
One God is our master, our saviour,
Who knows the hearts and minds of all.
Asleep we are carefree, awake we are carefree,
Because here and beyond, you abide O Lord!
Peace prevails at home,
Peace abounds outside,
Nanak says,
Because the Guru taught the practice.'

Guru Granth Sahib 1136

The same Sikh woman describes another passage that appeals to her. It describes God in terms of ordinary human relationships, as a parent, a friend, a saviour and as one who guides us:

'You are my father, you are my mother,
You are my kin, you are my brother,
You are my saviour everywhere.
Then why should I be afraid?
Through the help of your grace I
recognize you.
You are my shelter, you are my pride;
There is no other than you. The whole of
creation is your playground;
You create all beings
And allocate tasks as you will.
All is your doing, not ours.
By meditating on your name, gained
immense happiness;
By singing hymns of your attributes, found
supreme peace;
By the grace of the perfect Guru,
Nanak rejoices;
Congratulations are sung
When conflict is resolved.'

Guru Granth Sahib 103

Women who contributed to the Sikh faith

Guru Nanak's older sister, Bibi Nanki, is revered in Sikh history as a person who recognized Guru Nanak's divine message and presence. She also protected him countless times from their parents' wrath because he had chosen God's path and not the material path which his father, Mehta Kalu, followed. Mata Khivi, the wife of the second Guru, Guru Angad, firmly established the Sikh 'community kitchen', the **langar**. Bibi Bhani enjoys a very special place as the daughter of the third Guru, the wife of the fourth Guru and the mother of the fifth Guru.

Bibi Bhani, the young Arjan and Guru Amar Das

Her son, Guru Arjun, built the Harmandir Sahib, compiled the Granth Sahib and was the first martyr to religious persecution. The Sikh community is indebted to Bibi Bhani for ensuring the equal role of women in the Sikh faith. There are many other examples from the time of the Gurus of women taking on the role of key preachers.

People who may regard Sikhism in the same way as other eastern religions may find it unusual when they look more closely. Sometimes visitors to the gurdwara (the Sikh place of worship) are surprised to see a woman reciting from the Guru Granth Sahib. Both men and women have the same opportunity to study the scriptures and to participate in services.

God as male and female

As given in the example of the second hymn above, God is described both as mother and father. There are many such references in the scriptures. God has both male and female attributes, but is also without gender. Prayers are said remembering God as creator, sustainer and saviour. The human soul is described as female: both men and women have a female soul, which yearns to join the supreme soul, God, from whom it was separated at the time of birth.

Tasks

1   The Gurus said that godly company produces godly people; bad company produces evil people. What did they mean by this ? What are your views?

2   How have Sikh women contributed to the development of Sikh spirituality?

3   How can belief in God as father and mother help spiritual growth?

Congregational worship (diwan)

Sikhs gather at the gurdwara for prayers and for social activities. Though in most gurdwaras more people gather on Sundays, all days are of equal value. There are morning and evening prayer sessions.

The value of sangat (collective worship)

Much importance is attached to worship together as a community because Sikhs believe that the Guru resides in the sangat (congregration). The sangat is usually called satsangat ('assembly of the true') or sadhsangat ('assembly of the saints'). Guru Gobind Singh said to his followers: 'If anybody wants to see me, let him go to the sangat and approach it with faith and respect; he will surely see me there'.

Through the sangat the new disciple receives the Guru's instructions and acquires the qualities of sadhsangat through hearing the recitations from Guru Granth Sahib and singing and praying together, just as children learn from their parents. Bhai Gurdas, a devotee and relative of the Guru recounted the advantages of the sangat like this:

Ardas, the final prayer

'Trees that grow near the sandalwood become perfumed as sandal;
Metals touched by philosopher's stone become gold;
Rivers and streams going into the Ganga become the Ganga;
So does the sangat save sinners and wash away their sins,
Saves countless souls from the hell fires,
And the holy see God in there.'

The sangat is an example of an ideal community, in which the Guru resides. It encourages moral and spiritual values and helps in spiritual development.

The prayer sessions

The prayer session for the sangat is known as the diwan. This starts early in the morning and on a Sunday may finish in the afternoon any time after 2 p.m. The service consists of singing hymns from the Guru Granth Sahib with the accompaniment of drums (tabla), a harmonium or other types of instruments, such as dholki (two-sided drums), chimta (percussion

Disability is no barrier to paying respect to Guru Granth Sahib

Kirtan, the singing of hymns

instruments); then recitation from the Guru Granth Sahib, lectures on the lives and teachings of the gurus, sometimes a combination of music and discourse, and, to finish the session, the Ardas, the final prayer, with the congregation standing together. Then there is the sharing of karah parshad (a special sweet food), followed by the communal meal, langar, which is served to the whole congregation.

In the evening there is the recitation of rahras, the evening prayer, followed by hymn-singing by ragis (singers of devotional music). Then Kirtan Sohilla is recited, followed by Ardas. Finally, the Guru Granth Sahib is reverently laid to rest for the night. Most gurdwaras have a separate room for the resting place. The day comes to an end with remembrance of God and spiritual fulfilment.

Tasks

1   How does congregational worship help spiritual development for a Sikh?

2   Explain in your own words the meaning of the verse by Bhai Gurdas.

3   What can be achieved through prayer?

52 Sewa

Sewa, or service to the community, is a necessary part of a Sikh's life. It is a practical expression of the fostering of the Sikh spirit of giving and of service to fellow-beings, and a way of expressing love for God.

Types of sewa

There are three main types of sewa:

1 Manual, physical hard work, e.g. cleaning, washing, cooking, looking after shoes, fanning the congregation in hot weather, repair, maintenance and building work, etc. This is known as sewa with body (tan di sewa).

2 Service with the mind, e.g. reading the scriptures, telling stories about the lives of the gurus, looking after the Guru Granth Sahib, teaching about the Sikh way of life, etc. This is known as sewa with mind (man di sewa).

3 Service with wealth and resources (dhan di sewa).

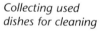

Collecting used dishes for cleaning

Looking after the shoes of worshippers

A Sikh may wish to serve the community in any of the above ways, or a combination of all three; for example, through donating labour, materials, food and money. You may see people helping in these various ways when you visit the gurdwara.

Langar

Whether the service is at home or in the gurdwara, there is a communal meal, langar, at the end of the prayer session. The Sikh tradition of free sharing of food was started by Guru Nanak to eliminate the barriers that existed between the rich and poor, the higher caste and the lower castes, the ruler and the ruled, and between men and women. Sikhs believe that all human beings are the children of God and are therefore equal as the offspring of the same parent.

The Mughal emperor shares langar

The Sikh tradition of 'equality in action' is very well illustrated by the story of the mighty Mughal emperor, Akbar. Akbar had heard about the preaching of the third guru, Guru Amardas, who was preaching for an ideal, God-loving and religious society, in which men and women had equal roles and everybody shared. Akbar came to visit the Guru with his royal army. He was told that the Guru could only see him after he had the langar, which was being served at the time. The emperor accepted the Guru's rule, sat on the floor with the poor and ordinary people and ate the food served to everybody. He was most impressed. After the meal, he was taken to the Guru's presence. He paid his respects and wished to make an offering of land. This was politely declined by the Guru, who said that the langar belonged to God and was made from the charity of the sangat.

The story of a young man

Another story relates to Guru Gobind Singh. One day the Guru was sitting with his followers and preaching to them the teachings of the gurus and the importance of service to others. During the conversation he asked for a drink of water. One young Sikh got up and offered to fetch some water. He went out and soon brought a glass of water and presented it to the Guru. While the Guru was taking the glass from the young man, he noticed that he had very soft hands. He said: 'Your hands look very soft to me. Why is that?' At this, the father of the young man rose and replied: 'Today is the first time that he has done something for another person and I am very pleased that you have had such an effect on him'. The Guru remarked: 'I like to take my drink of water from the person whose hands serve others, and not the one who does not serve anybody at all.'

The Guru wanted the Sikhs to be ready and willing to serve. This selfless service can be seen in action in the gurdwaras.

Langar being served

Second helpings of food!

Bhai Kanhayya

Sewa is not limited to the gurdwara and serving Sikhs. There are medical and healing centres in India, where medicine is dispensed free of charge to the needy, and there are Sikh-run hospitals and care centres for those who are not supported in the community (this is particularly true of leprosy victims). The Sikh version of the Red Cross owes its inspiration to Bhai Kanhayya.

Bhai Kanhayya was a disciple of Guru Gobind Singh. There was a battle between the Guru's small army and the mighty Mughal force. There were many wounded and dying in the field, crying for water to relieve their thirst. Bhai Kanhayya started serving water to everybody who needed it, on both sides. This made the fighting Sikhs very angry, because they felt that Bhai Kanhayya was helping the enemy maintain their strength. Some of them reported Bhai Kanhayya to the Guru. The Guru asked him to explain his action. Bhai Kanhayya replied: 'I don't see any friend or foe. I only see you demanding water, my Lord.' The Guru was so pleased with Bhai Kanhayya that he gave him ointment to tend the wounds, as well. In this way the Sikh Red Cross was created.

Tasks

1 How can sewa encourage spiritual development?

2 Why is langar an important form of sewa?

3 Explain the meaning behind the story of Akbar.

4 What spiritual lesson can be learnt from the story of the young man?

5 What does the story of Bhai Kanhayya teach us?

53 The Khalsa and the importance of Amrit

The word Khalsa is used to describe the community of Sikhs who observe the physical and religious symbols of the faith. It is the aspiration of every believing Sikh to become a Khalsa Sikh. It is a step towards spiritual fulfilment.

There are three broad types of Sikhs: the Sahajdhari Sikhs, the Kesadhari Sikhs and the Amritdhari Sikhs.

Sahajdhari Sikhs

The word Sahajdhari means 'one who is slowly moving towards the Sikh path'. Sahajdhari Sikhs belive in the teachings of the gurus. They may attend the gurdwara and observe the traditions of Sikh service, but they do not observe the physical rules of observation, such as wearing the five symbols (see below). Men are usually clean-shaven and women may cut their hair.

Kesadhari Sikhs

The word Kesadhari literally means 'one who wears hair'. In addition to the main Sikh beliefs, Kesadhari Sikhs maintain some or all of the symbols of the faith. They maintain their hair as it grows naturally: scissors or knives do not touch their hair. Many Sikhs remain Kesadhari Sikhs.

Amritdhari Sikhs

The ultimate condition for perfection is to be an Amritdhari Sikh. This literally means 'one who has taken Amrit' (a special nectar). The Amritdhari Sikh is the Khalsa Sikh: one who maintains the physical and religious symbols of the faith and leads his or her life according to the teachings of the gurus; prays in the mornings and evenings and before bed time, and remembers God in his or her daily activities. Khalsa Sikhs feel that their relationship with God is a special one spiritually.

The creation of the Khalsa by Guru Gobind Singh

The purpose of the Khalsa

The Khalsa was started by Guru Gobind Singh on Baisakhi Day at Anandpur in the Punjab in India, in 1699. This day is now known as the birthday of the Khalsa and is also New Year's Day for Sikhs. The Guru's purpose in creating the Khalsa was to form a community of 'saint soldiers' who had moral courage, faith, compassion and majesty. They were to be a community of equals, among whom the barriers of race, caste, gender and region would not exist. They would be prepared to fight injustice and persecution and defend the weak and humble at any time.

Why become an Amritdhari Sikh?

Here is one Sikh's account of why he became an Amritdhari Sikh three years ago:

'I came to England 28 years ago. I had to give up my Sikh form – cut off my hair and take off my turban – in order to get a suitable job, appropriate to my profession. But I was very unhappy in my personal life for a number of years. A few years back my daughter's marriage failed. Things around me became very hard: my business, my work, relatives all seemed to get me down. I had no satisfaction. I became very ▶

Amrit being prepared

In order to maintain the special form, the five K symbols are worn with pride. They are:

- natural uncut hair (kes)
- a wooden comb (kangha)
- a steel bracelet (kara)
- a small sword (kirpan)
- a pair of specially tailored briefs (kachera).

Men, and sometimes women, wear the first two symbols under the turban.

It is the wish of a devoted Sikh to be in the presence of the Guru and to be able to live up to the teachings of the Guru. When, on Baisakhi Day, initiation ceremonies take place, Sikhs feel a unity in spirit with the Guru.

depressed. Then I started going to the gurdwara every Sunday and prayed daily, but I still felt that I was not contented. I shared my concerns with the Granthi (who looks after the gurdwara and provides religious pastoral support), who encouraged me to become an Amritdhari.

I thought about it and decided to go through the Amrit ceremony. As preparation, I began to grow my hair and beard and over a period began to wear my turban.

I decided to take Amrit at Bibi Nanki's gurdwara in Birmingham. On the appointed day, I bathed myself completely and washed my hair. I wore the **five K symbols** and drove from my home in East London to Birmingham, by myself.

There were 25 other people, men and women, who had also come from different parts of the country to become Amritdhari Sikhs.

The Amrit was prepared by five Sikhs who said five prayers while stirring the sugar crystals in water, and then we received it. It was a wonderful day. I felt very inspired and much closer to the Guru.

That was three years ago. Now I feel much better. I feel at peace with myself, and am able to deal with any situation. I feel I am spiritually a much stronger person.'

An Amritdhari Sikh wears symbols with pride

Why Khalsa is important

In his writings about the Khalsa, Guru Gobind Singh says:

'Khalsa is my special form;
Khalsa is where I reside.'

Tasks

1 How can a 'saint soldier' be spiritually developed?

2 What lesson can be learnt from the story of the man who chose to be initiated?

3 Explain the meaning of the two verses of Guru Gobind Singh about the Khalsa.

4 What is the purpose of celebrating Baisakhi Day?

5 What are the five K symbols?

The origins of Jainism

India is rich in religious variety. About 2,500 years ago there lived a man called Vardhamana. His followers renamed him **Mahavira**, the Great Hero. They believed him to be the 24th and last pathfinder, or guide, showing the way to happiness and bliss for all living beings. Jains call them Tirthankara. These 24 people (one was a woman) were also called **jinas**, or spiritual victors: people who had conquered themselves. From the word 'jina' came Jain, the name which is given to the religion on which about twelve million people base their lives today.

Mahavira was born in about 599 BCE and died in 527 BCE. At the age of about 30, when his parents had died, he left home and became a monk. He lived a very strict life, eating little, keeping silent for long periods of time to purify his speech, and meditating intensely to purify his mind. In this way he became detached from the consequences of his past lives and of his present one. (Mahavira believed in rebirth, but he did not believe, like most of the people of his day, that there were gods who could help him to a better birth.) After twelve years, Mahavira became an enlightened being, a jina, conqueror of the self, through his own efforts.

Mahavira taught for 30 more years, right up to the moment of his death. He died after meditating and fasting for two days.

Mahavira's teachings

The key to Mahavira's teaching, which Jains believe should be followed by anyone desiring enlightenment or spiritual liberation, are summed up in this sentence:

> 'There is nothing so small and subtle as the soul, nor any element so vast in space. Similarly, there is no quality of the soul more subtle than non-violence and no virtue of spirit greater than reverence for life (ahimsa)'.

Ahimsa, he said means: 'Do not injure, abuse, oppress, insult, torment, torture or kill any living beings'. The Jain tradition teaches: 'Ahimsa para dharmah' – 'Non-violence is the supreme religion'. All souls are equal, irrespective of class, creed, gender or species, and all have the potential for spiritual growth.

Spirituality is not an individual matter

Many Indians share something of the view of ahimsa. It is interesting to see a student in a

Respect for all life means that a Jain monk will use a mask and brush to avoid killing life forms

classroom catch a wasp or some other insect which many of us fear because of its bite or sting. The Indian student will put it in a handkerchief, being careful not to harm it, take it to the door or window and release it into the open without any fuss.

Jains often go even further than their Hindu or Buddhist neighbours, who might be equally concerned not to injure creatures. The photo shows a Jain monk with his mouth covered. This is to make sure that he doesn't even harm tiny living beings in the air by his warm breath. He may also be seen sweeping a brush in front of him when he sees small insects. A beetle or spider might be on the path, and he does not want to tread on it. Most people in India understand the Jain view, even if they do not share it to the same extent, and they behave respectfully towards Jains. Some westerners, when they first see Jains behaving this way, may be amused and are sometimes rude. If they were to ask a mask-wearing, brush-carrying Jain to explain their actions, the Jain might reply that all life is precious and living beings are bound together by mutual support and interdependence. Mahavira said:

> **'One who neglects or disregards the existence of earth, air, fire, water, and vegetation disregards his own existence which is entwined with them.'**

In other words, what we do affects others, even animals, and what they do affects us. Cruelty – even damaging a plant unnecessarily – harms us as much as the plant.

Jains should be strict vegetarians, eating no meat or fish, and no eggs. They live on vegetables, cereals and milk products.

Spiritual freedom

The way of self-denial, or asceticism, which a Jain should follow could seem selfish, but it is not. Jain ascetics progress on a spiritual path; they have friendship to all and malice to none. The Jain code of conduct has five vows:

- Non-violence, not only in conduct but in thought and word. One should not think or speak in a way which is hurtful and harmful to others – and ahimsa applies as much to animals as humans.

- Seeking truth and speaking it, though not with the intention of being hurtful.

- Behaving honestly and never taking anything by force or theft. Many Jains become bankers or lawyers because people know that they can trust them with their affairs.

- Self-control. Jains should control their sensual pleasures and should be respectful of others.

- Jains should not be greedy and covet the belongings of others.

Jain spirituality is practical. Jains study the teachings of the Tirthankaras, which are found in their scriptures, and they meditate upon them, but most of all they must live moral lives, especially keeping the principle of ahimsa. Liberation or spiritual freedom is a state of eternal bliss, free from the bondage of matter, but beyond description: it can only be experienced.

Tasks

1. What do Jains mean when they say: 'Take your cue from the bee, which sucks honey in the blossoms of a tree without hurting the blossom and strengthens itself'?

2. 'I only carved my name on the bark of a tree, what's wrong with that?' What reply might a Jain give?

3. Why are many Jains active environmentalists?

55 / Baha'is

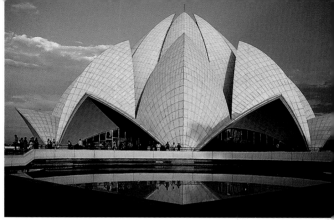

Baha'i house of worship, New Delhi, India. Baha'is like to relate their buildings to the local culture

The origins of Baha'i teaching

The Baha'i faith is one of the world's youngest religions. In 1817 a child was born in Tehran in Persia (now in Iran) and was given the name Mirza Husayn Ali. He is better known as **Baha'u'llah**, an Arabic phrase which means 'Glory of God'. His father was a minister in the court of the Shah, the ruler of Persia. Mirza Husayn Ali married young, as was the custom of the time, and he and his wife gave much of their time to helping the poor. They were popularly known as 'The Father and Mother of the poor'.

When he was 27 Mirza Husayn Ali began to follow a famous teacher called the Bab. They wrote to one another, but never met. The Bab sent Mirza Husayn Ali all his pens and papers, indicating that he should continue the Bab's work. He also had the scroll of his writings smuggled to him before he was executed.

Two years later some Babis, followers of the Bab tried to kill the Shah. They failed. All disciples who could be found were rounded up and put in prison. Among them was Mirza Husayn Ali.

The divine revelation

The Bab had foretold that God was sending a special messenger. Mirza Husayn Ali became aware that he was the promised one during a mystical experience while he was in prison. This is how he described it in a letter to the Shah some years later:

> 'During the days that I lay in the Tehran prison, though the galling weight of the chains and the stench-filled air allowed me but little sleep, still in those infrequent moments of slumber I felt as if something flowed from the crown of my head over my breast, even as a mighty torrent that pours itself upon the earth from the summit of a lofty mountain. Every limb of ▶

> ▶ my body would, as a result, be set afire. At such moments my tongue recited what no man could bear. O King! I was only a man like others, asleep upon my bed, when the breezes of the All-Glorious wafted over me, and taught me the knowledge of all that had been. This thing is not from me but from he who is Almighty and All-Knowing. And he bade me lift up my voice between earth and heaven, and for this there befell me what has caused the tears of everyone to flow ... His all-compelling summons has reached me, and caused me to speak his praise among all people.'

Baha'u'llah's journeys

No evidence of his implication in the plot to kill the Shah could be brought against Baha'u'llah, as he was now being called. Nevertheless he was imprisoned. When a Russian minister at the Shah's court used his influence to get Baha'u'llah released, the Shah agreed and Baha'u'llah was banished from Persia. His property and all his wealth were taken from him. He, his pregnant wife Navvab and their children made a three-month journey to Baghdad in Iraq, living on the little money which Navvab could raise from selling the silver buttons on her dresses.

During the next few years Baha'u'llah wrote letters to many world rulers. In his letter to Queen Victoria, he wrote:

> 'The sovereign remedy and mightiest instrument which the Lord has ordained for ▶

► the healing of all the world is the union of all its people in one universal cause, one common faith. This can be achieved in no way except through the power of a skilled and all-powerful and inspired physician.'

He was not, of course writing about himself, but God, though he was saying that his message was the one which would lead to the healing of the nations. Queen Victoria's comment was: 'If this is of God, it will endure. If not, no harm can come of it'.

Baha'u'llah was banished to Akka (Acre) in Palestine (now Israel) in 1868. He was released from house arrest and went to live in nearby Haifa, where he died in 1892. His tomb has become a pilgrimage site for Baha'is. There are now about 12 million Baha'is, living in almost every country in the world.

The Baha'i message

The key teaching of the Baha'is is that humankind is one. Baha'u'llah wrote:

'There can be no doubt whatever that the people of the world, of whatever race or religion, derive their inspiration from one heavenly source and are the subject of one God.'

His son put it this way:

'All people are leaves and fruits of the same tree. They all have the same origin. The same rain has fallen upon them all, the same sun makes them grow, they are all refreshed by the same breeze. The whole of humanity is enveloped by the Mercy and the Grace of God. As the Holy Writings tell us: "All are equal before God. He is no respecter of persons".'

Baha'is believe that evil is the absence of good, in the same way that darkness is the absence of light. It can be avoided by obeying God's will. Fasting can strengthen spiritual development, and from 2 to 20 March every year, Baha'is fast from sunrise to sunset.

Equality of the sexes is essential, according to Baha'is if the world is to be truly united in a just world order. Their writings say:

'The world of humanity has two wings – one is women, the other men. Not until both wings are equally developed can the bird fly.'

Baha'is do not become involved in party politics, but support peace movements like the United Nations.

Baha'u'llah himself said:

'We have come to unite and weld together all who dwell on earth.'

Tasks

1   What evidence do you think Baha'is might put forward to support the view that: 'As long as women are prevented from attaining their highest possibilities, so long will men be unable to achieve the greatness which might be theirs'?

2   Discuss the importance (a) for Baha'u'llah and (b) for his followers of his awareness of being called by God to be his messenger.

3   Baha'u'llah said: 'Let your visions be world-embracing rather than confined to your own selves'. What is needed in practical terms if someone wishes to have this worldwide vision?

Australian Aborigines

Perhaps the oldest living religions of the world are those of the different clans of the Australian Aborigines. When white men arrived in Australia in 1788 they found about 350,000 people already living there – people known as Aborigines. They had come from Indonesia, Papua, and other islands to the north of Australia between 100,000 and 40,000 years earlier.

Clash of cultures

It quickly became clear that the cultures of the Aborigines and the British who began to settle the continent would not mix. The Europeans were farmers and prospectors for gold and other minerals. The Aborigines were food-gatherers, fishermen and hunters, using the dingo (a kind of dog which they had brought with them) and boomerangs and other hunting tools. The ways of the Aborigines and the settlers were so different that a Roman Catholic priest once referred to them as the only race he had come across who had 'no religion'. He was wrong, but what he said was convenient, for it enabled white people to suggest that Aborigines had no souls, and were not, in fact, human.

The Creator in the form of rain gods which face east so that they can see the light where they were born

It was not until 1967 that Aborigines were included in Australian population statistics. Meanwhile their population had shrunk to about 40,000 pure Aborigines and another 100,000 of mixed blood.

That Aborigines survived at all says much for their character. Some of them were hunted like kangaroos and other animals; some killed themselves rather than become virtual slaves to the white farmers; the children of others were taken away from their parents by missionaries, adopted and brought up in communities as Europeans.

The Aborigine tradition

Aboriginal spirituality did exist but was very different from the Christianity of the white people. It was closely linked with the land. For human survival the Aborigines depended upon nature, access to animals, fruit and fresh water. They moved around their clan territories from season to season, as nomads. Their religious stories brought out their oneness with the areas in which they lived, and taught clan morality, such as respect for elders and for female members of the extended family. Here is one of their stories:

> 'A great man, Angamunggi, was treacherously killed by his son, who had already committed incest with his sisters. The son, Tjinimin, was filled with guile, malice and lust. Having already seduced his sisters, he next speared his father while he was surrounded by his children, enjoying a festive moment at the gathering of the clans. In agony and about to die, the father nevertheless lingered on to perform a series of marvels. He moved from place to place, and in doing so formed a track which is now sacred. At each resting place he tried without success to staunch the flow of blood from the spear wound in his side. In some mysterious way his blood produced perennial pools and springs of water, which remain to this day as

Aboriginal traditions live on through the work of modern artists

need to re-experience their unity with the spiritual world.

The story of Angamunggi is a story of the **Dream Time,** the period of creation which, some Aborigines say, came to an end with the coming of the white man. The whites spoke of Aborigines who were farm labourers and left their work, 'going walkabout', saying that they were lazy and unreliable; but the Aborigines had different priorities in life. They were living out their religious stories.

New attitudes

During the 20th century attempts were made to understand and find a place for the Aborigines in Australia, but it was not until 1967 that they were given civil rights, among which was the right to vote, to own land, and to bring cases against any white Australians who oppressed them.

his marks or signs upon the land. After a long trek he took all the fire present in the world, tied it to his head with his own hair, and waded into the sea. At the last moment another man courageously snatched a brand from his head just as Angamunggi was about to disappear beneath the waves. In this way fire was saved for men, who would otherwise have been forced to eat raw food, like animals. Even in his death agonies, however, Angamunggi had given men perennial, life-giving waters, in which he also placed the spirits of all those children who have been born since then.'

The sacred journey, the **Dream Journey,** is one which all Aborigines go on, first when they become initiated members of the clan, and afterwards at times when they feel the

Tasks

1   Discuss the clash between the culture and spirituality of the white men and the Aborigines.

2   How might it change the way we think about the world and behave if we believed that the Earth has a sacred dimension?

3   What feelings do you think a clan would have had when it found the sacred land, through which it experienced the Dream Time, fenced off by farmers, so that it could no longer make the Journey?

The pre-European legacy

Every continent had its inhabitants long before European settlers went there, and Africa is no exception. We know much about the dead religion of the ancient Egyptians, because they have interested Europeans since the time of the ancient Greeks and Romans, and their writings exist. One of Napoleon's scholars broke the code of the hieroglyphics which the ancient Egyptians used, and since then even more has been known about them.

But Africa has many other peoples, most of whom still have an awareness of their tribes, even though their ancestors were taken as slaves to north America. At the end of the 19th century, Britain, France, Belgium and Germany carved up the continent along lines of latitude and longitude, ignoring tribal boundaries. Sometimes members of one group might live in

Map of Africa showing where some of the living primal religions are to be found

three different countries. Only Ethiopia escaped colonization, because it was a Christian country, of forbidding mountains. However, in the 1930s even Ethiopia was conquered, by Italy.

With the imperialists came the missionaries. It is a bitter African joke that the missionaries taught them to pray with their eyes closed, the Christian way. When they opened their eyes the missionaries had taken their land and given them the Bible!

However, these native Africans already had their own religions, and some of them survive into present times. There are many of these religions, but here are some of the aspects they share.

Tribal views of God

African spirituality was of a tribal rather than an individual kind, and was not contained in books: in their cultures there was no need for writing. In the compact tribe, everything passed by word of mouth.

Here is one of their prayers:

'In the beginning was God,
Today is God,
Tomorrow will be God.
Who can make an image of God?
He has no body.
He is a word which comes from your mouth.
That word! It is no more,
It is past, and still it lives!
So is God.'

A tribe of Zaire

Sometimes doubt or unhappiness makes people feel that God does not exist or care. But he does, according to the Dinka tribe of the Sudan:

'Truly God the creator is there
And we say: Far off is the Father,
the Father up there.
God the creator is near,
And we say: he is not here.'

African divine healer who mediates God's power to cure the sick

The spirit world

Many people believe that the spirit world is around them, as this prayer, offered at burial by the Ashanti of Ghana, reminds believers:

> 'The spirits of the dead are thronging together
> Like mosquitoes in the evening.
> Like swarms of mosquitoes dancing
> in the evening, When the sky has turned
> black, entirely black.
> Like whirling leaves, dead leaves in the wind,
> Dead leaves in the wind.
> They wait for him who will come and say:
> "Come" to the one, and "Go" to the other.
> And God will be with his children.
> And God will be with his children.'

God's favours

Many African religions teach that God's power may be given to special people. In the West these people are often called 'medicine men' or even 'witch doctors', because healing is one of the gifts which they have received. A prayer by one of these men, of the Barundi tribe of Burundi is:

> 'Ruler of strength, spirit of virile energy,
> You can do all, without you I am powerless;
> I who am consecrated to you, I who am
> pledged to you,
> O spirit, I get my strength and power from
> you. You brought me the gift.
> Spirit of force come to me. Acknowledge my
> call, come! Come!'

God's punishments

Most religions describe how God is loving, but sometimes his people will not listen to him or even think of him, so disaster befalls them like a curse; and most religions have stories of far-off times to warn people against such heedlessness. Believers may take such stories at their face value or regard them as metaphors: God is love; without God love cannot be enjoyed, so there is no real success and happiness.

> 'Some awful curse will descend on us,
> Like the curse that descended in far-off times.
> So speaks the creator of men,
> But men refuse to listen.
> Some awful curse will descend on us,
> Like the curse that descended in far-off times.
> We have but one word to say:
> Idle about! Sink into slothfulness!
> Such men will gain nothing from the Father,
> For they do not know his voice.
> He is the one who loves man.'

Tasks

1 How might the bereaved find comfort in the Ashanti prayer for the dead?

2 Discuss the Zaire prayer which says that God is like a word which is past but still lives. What do you think it means?

3 What ideas of God can you find in the prayers in this spread?

117

Native Americans and the colonies

Christopher Columbus did not find America: it was never lost! However, the European conquerors, or Conquistadors, as they were called, soon overwhelmed the native Aztec and Inca empires and made South America Spanish and Portuguese.

North America was colonized mainly by the British and French, who also encountered existing inhabitants. Like those in South America, they had originally come from Siberia, many centuries earlier. Sometimes treaties were made with these people. That which members of The Society of Friends made with Native Americans and their colony of Pennsylvania was never broken, but most of the rest were.

After independence

The British colonies won their independence in 1776 and declared themselves to be the United States of America. Since then more Europeans, not only Britons, have settled in the country. The need for land increased and they began to push westwards and take land from its original occupants. The Native Americans were squeezed into reservations and left with the land which the new settlers did not want. Often it was too poor to cultivate. The reservations were far from the sites of their ancestors and their holy places.

Two things made the plight of the Native Americans even worse. One was the buffalo trade. Many Native Americans were nomads, who relied on the buffalo for food. They killed only what they needed. But the white settlers hunted them for trade, and soon the Native Americans were threatened with starvation, as the number of buffalo declined.

Also, white prospectors found gold in the land where the Native Americans had been allowed to remain. They were moved on by force to even poorer land. From about 1835 the Native Americans who resisted the United States' army were hunted like animals. The whites often called them 'savages' and stories were sent back to Washington DC, the capital of the USA, about the cruel things they did. Actually, they were usually only trying to protect themselves.

Reconstruction of an exterior and interior of an Iroquois long house, Ontario, Canada. Native Americans raised crops here and kept cattle

These Native Americans are the people you may know better as 'Redskins' or 'Red Indians'. You may have seen them on films, depicted as savage trouble-makers. Nowadays they are called Native Americans – because that is what they are – and films often show them in a more honest light, as a persecuted minority. They fall into many groups, with different lifestyles. Some were nomads using teepees; others stayed in one place and grew crops, such as maize or 'Indian corn'. Their religious lives also varied so here we can only outline a few of their teachings and spiritual ideas.

Native American prayers

'Oh, Great Spirit, whose voice I hear in the wind,
Whose breath gives life to the world, hear me.
I come to you as one of your many children.
I am small and weak.
I need your strength and your wisdom.
May I walk in your beauty.
Make my eyes be ever ready to behold the red and purple sunset.
Make my hands respect the things you have made.
Make my ears sharp to hear your voice.
Make me wise so that I may know the things you taught your children,
The lessons you have written in every leaf and rock.
Make me forever strong, not to be superior to my brothers and sisters, but to fight my greatest enemy – myself.
Make me ready to come to you with straight eyes,
So that when life fades as the fading sunset,
My spirit may come to you without shame.'

Originally translated by Chief Yellow Lark, a Sioux, 1887

'The creator asks only that we honour the life we are given, by:
giving thanks for the winds, the waters, the sun and the land,
honouring the elders;
honouring the elder brother/sister spirits;
honouring woman spirit;
keeping promises – hold your pledges;
being kind – use your gifts and dreams for good purpose;
being peaceful – temper your thoughts, passions, words and deeds;
being courageous – the more you know, the more you trust, the less you fear;
moderate your dreams, thoughts, words and deeds;
listen and watch – someday you will be wise.
The above actions will deem you a "Person of Peace".'

Some Native American young people treasure these Seven Teachings and try to follow them:

'To cherish knowledge is to know wisdom.
To know love is to know peace.
To honour all creation is to have respect.
Courage is to face life with integrity.
Honesty in facing a situation is to be brave.
Humility is to know yourself as a sacred part of creation.
Truth is to know all these things.

Tasks

1   What ideas did you have about Native Americans before you read this unit? Have your ideas now altered in some way? If so, how?

2   When you next see a re-run of an old Western on TV, think about the way in which the Native Americans are portrayed. How fair and accurate is it?

3   In the first prayer the person who offers it says that God has written lessons in every leaf and rock. What do you think they have in mind? What lessons might we learn from leaves or rocks? Explain what is meant in this prayer by the line: 'Make me ready to come to you with straight eyes'.

4   Discuss the meaning and value the Seven Teachings might have for you and your community.

Not everybody believes in something, despite all the beliefs described in this book. Some say there is no spirituality now, and none in eternity.

Albert Meltzer

Albert Meltzer died in May 1996. He was an anarchist – a man who was against organized society and certainly organized religion and an organized universe. He didn't like governments and didn't believe in God. He was a popular man: a crowd followed his coffin from his home to the crematorium in Lewisham, London. The hearse was drawn by two horses. Among the mourners who followed were men with pony tails, veterans who had fought in the Spanish Civil War in the 1930s, young white Rastas with eighteen-hole Doc Marten boots and a Southern Reggae Jazz band. Albert Meltzer had been an anarchist since he was 15. He had fought against the Nazi Blackshirts of Sir Oswald Moseley as they tried to march down Cable Street, in the east end of London, and cause trouble for the Jews. He had helped Germans who opposed Hitler before World War II.

Albert Meltzer made plans for his funeral, which he wanted to be dignified. His last requests were:

> 'I want to die in dignity but have my passing celebrated with jollity. I've told my executors that I want a stand-up comedian in the pulpit telling amusing anecdotes, and the coffin to slide into the incinerator to the sound of Marlene Dietrich.'

A comedian called Noel James told some stories and then the coffin disappeared from view to Marlene Dietrich singing 'See what the boys in the back room will have'. Another song was sung – 'They call me Al' – and finally a video was shown of Al Meltzer laughing fit to burst, while someone tried to interview him.

Everyone laughed, but as they left the crematorium some were crying, completely against his wishes and directions. He had said:

> 'Anyone mourning should be denounced as the representative of a credit card company and thrown out on their ear.'

When people die, their debts die with them – hence the tears of a credit card company representative!

The funeral of Albert Meltzer, anarchist and supporter of human rights

Making choices

Albert Meltzer seemed to believe that spirituality was making people happy and sticking your tongue out at authority. However, he also wrote:

> 'If I have miscalculated and there really is a God, I'd like to feel if he's got any sense of humour or feeling for humanity, there's no one he'd sooner have in heaven than people like me. And if he hasn't, who wants in?'

Perhaps he was thinking of what a comedian once said – Groucho Marx – when someone was telling him he couldn't become a member of a club because he was a Jew: 'That doesn't matter – if there is a club lousy enough to allow me to join it, I wouldn't want to be a member!'

Albert Meltzer didn't seem to care whether he came to a dead end or not, but he certainly decided how he should live.

Journeys

Four couples met in a pub in Reading and decided that they would each set out upon a journey and return in three years to share their experiences. If they couldn't make it back, they agreed to write a letter for the landlady to give to the rest.

The evening for their reunion came, but there was no sign of the couples. But there were four letters. The landlady decided to open them and read them with her partner. The first letter was postmarked Cairns in Australia:

> 'Hi! We won't be back because we've got a job teaching people to scuba-dive on the Coral Reef. What about coming to join us? By the way, Mavis had twin girls last year!'

The second letter came from South Africa. It read:

> 'You know how South Africa changed when Nelson Mandela became President. Well we thought we would go and see what it is like. Harry started this club for youngsters in a ▶

▶ township to help them learn sport and I work as a nurse visiting folk in their homes. So we shall not be back. Sorry I haven't time to write more. Love Iris.
>
> PS You're welcome any time but be ready to work!'

From San Francisco came this brief note:

> 'This is the life! Sailing, swimming, fishing, the GOOD LIFE! Pity you can't be here! ... and that we haven't time to get back. But who knows how long this will last? Got to enjoy life while you can. Beth and Chuck.'

The last envelope came from London, no distance at all from Reading. It was from Heather and Steve. It looked a bit grubby and not at all interesting. It read:

> 'Well, we must be the failures. We got no further than Paddington, where we came across this chap sleeping rough. We decided to look after him for a few days. When we cleaned him up he turned out to be quite young, in his 20s. But he was on drugs and was HIV pos., so no one wanted to know him. He got a job but was never able to live by himself so he is with us. We didn't have to go far for our journey, did we?'

Tasks

1 Imagine that the four couples eventually meet up a year later. Divide your class into groups of eight and role-play the discussion they might have held about which was the most successful and the most spiritual journey. Share the main points which each group made with the rest of the class.

2 Write a poem or a song called *Life's Journey*.

3 What is the message of Albert Meltzer's funeral?

121

Gaia Consciousness

A view of the Earth rising over the edge of the moon, taken from Apollo II

A new view of the world

In 1969 the Apollo spacecraft embarked upon a successful mission to land a man on the moon. One of the crew, Bill Anders, looked in the other direction and saw the Earth as no one had ever seen it before. He said:

'We've come all this way to explore the moon, and the most important thing is that we've discovered the Earth.

He saw the Earth as it is in our photograph: an earth with no national frontiers, no wars, no different races and religions: just Planet Earth, land and sea intermingled and enfolded in swirling cloud. It look like a marble that children play with, of mixed colours, floating in darkness.

Some people were already thinking of a New Age, the Age of Aquarius, which would, somewhere between then and 2062, replace the old, fading, exhausted Age of Pisces, which had

lasted for about 2,000 years. This discovery of the Earth gave one form to a New Age Movement which has many aspects, and which has influenced some existing religions, especially Christianity. Of course, if you have read the units on the Aborigines or Native Americans you will realize that the discovery of Earth in 1969 was really no more than rediscovering a precious teaching which some people had never forgotten.

The Gaia Movement

The particular movement relating to the earth came to be known as **Gaia Consciousness**. Gaia is the name of the earth goddess of the ancient Greeks. By giving the Earth such a name, the movement was making the important statement that the Earth is alive.

A scientist, Dr James Lovelock, put forward the Gaia hypothesis. This is a the theory that the Earth is a living organism, as much as human beings and animals are. It fights against the diseases which humankind inflicts upon it, such as the destruction of forests and the pollution of rivers. Sometimes it manages to win, as we see when a pit heap becomes a grassy hill without human aid, or a quarry turns into a lake which attracts wildlife to its shores and its waters. Archaeologists frequently discover the ruins of Roman forts and villas or medieval villages which their inhabitants left to decay into ruins and which the Earth covered over to become a field or a woodland. Dr Lovelock noticed, however, that the story was often one of the Earth becoming filled with rubbish, like an empty skip left in a city street.

Calls for action

Governments met at Rio de Janeiro in Brazil some years ago and agreed that something must be done about those things which were killing the world, such as the destruction of the ozone layer, the cutting down of forests and over-fishing the ocean's limited resources; but little seems to have happened as a result. Every country seems to be waiting for others to act.

The prospect of a silent spring, with no birdsong, was predicted 25 years ago. As skylarks, curlews, lapwings and other species of birds diminish in numbers, there is a fear that it may not be far away. Even the coughing of starlings and pigeons trying to breathe in our polluted cities may soon be a thing of the past!

Women and Gaia Consciousness

Women are particularly involved in New Age movements and Gaia Consciousness. They make up half of the world's human beings, giving birth to men only to see them killed in wars. They feel the pain of the Earth. They became frustrated with talk.

In 1982 an American painter, Helene Aylon, decided upon one symbolic action. She organized a visit to twelve Strategic Air Command weapons sites in the USA – places where nuclear weapons are stored. She took an Earth Ambulance, a converted medical corps vehicle, and went from place to place

There are many New Age movements and centres. One is the Findhorn Community, founded in 1965. They believe that through meditation they can develop and strengthen the spiritual relationship between themselves and the Earth

gathering earth in pillows: 800 bags full. As she travelled, she collected pillows given by people near the weapons bases. They wrote on the sacks about their dreams and nightmares about the fate of the Earth.

Finally, the earth-filled pillow cases were taken to the United Nations and carried into the square outside, named after a great secretary-general, Dag Hammarskjold, on army stretchers.

In 1985 sacks filled with sand from Hiroshima and Nagasaki were covered with messages written by the hibakushas, Japanese women who had survived when the atomic bombs were dropped on their cities in 1945.

Many more symbolic acts may be needed before governments really take Gaia hypothesis seriously. Most people seem to think that the Earth, which has been about for millions of years, always will be, and that human beings can use it in any way they like.

Tasks

1   Discuss the view that the Earth is alive.

2   How might it help humanity if we believed that the Earth is our mother?

3   Consider the belief that spirituality is more than saying prayers and meditating: it is seeing the world and all its inhabitants in a spiritual way.

Glossary

Adhan the call to **salah**, prayer. [Islam]

Agnostic a person who doubts the existence of a god or gods, or of the supernatural. The word was coined by T H Huxley in 1869 from the prefix 'a' (without) and 'gnostic' (good at knowing). Its meaning, therefore, is 'without knowledge'. [Humanism]

Ahimsa non-violence [Jainism and Hinduism]

Ahl-al-suffah poor companions of the Prophet Muhammad, who lived in the mosque at **Madinah.** Their name is derived from the Arabic word 'suffa' which was the raised platform on which they resided. This is the origin of the English word sofa. [Islam]

Akhirah the hereafter. For Muslims this comprises a belief in the Day of Judgment and life after death. [Islam]

Al-hamdu-li-Llah an Arabic term meaning 'Thanks to God'. [Islam]

Allahu akbar an Arabic term meaning 'God is great'. [Islam]

Arafat a plain outside Makkah where pilgrims gather during hajj. [Islam]

Arkan an Arabic term meaning pillar, used to describe the fundamental principles upon which Islam is built. [Islam]

Asana set postures such as sitting; connected with the practice of yoga. [Hinduism]

Aum the sacred syllable, representing the Supreme Being and eternal truth. Most prayers begin and end with the recitation of this syllable. [Hinduism]

Baha'u'llah 'Glory of God'. The name given to Mirza Husayn Ali (1817-1892 CE), the founder of the Baha'is faith. [Baha' is]

Barakah an Arabic term meaning Allah's blessings. [Islam]

Bismillah-ir-Rahman-ir-Rahim an Arabic phrase meaning 'In the name of God, the Gracious, the Merciful'. [Islam]

Brahman the Supreme Spirit, God. [Hinduism]

Bukhari Muhammad b. Isma'il al-Bukhari, compiler of the **hadith.** [Islam]

Darshan 'viewing', catching a glimpse of a **deity**; to be in the presence of God at a sacred shrine or a place of pilgrimage. [Hinduism]

Deity a manifestation of the enlightened mind. Used as a focus for prayer and meditation, they appear in many different forms to help human and other beings. [Buddhism]

Dharma the religious and moral duties of a Hindu based on age, family and social position within a community. [Hinduism]

Dhikr the practice of repeating Allah's name or attributes. [Islam]

Dhul Hijjah the month of hajj, the twelfth month of the Muslim calendar. [Islam]

Dream journey the sacred journey Australian Aborigines go on, first when they become initiated members of the clan, and afterwards at times when they feel the need to re-experience their unity with the spiritual world. [Aborigines]

Dream time the period of creation, which some Australian Aborigines say came to an end with the coming of the white man. [Aborigines]

Du'a supplication or private prayer. [Islam]

Five books of Moses Genesis, Exodus, Leviticus, Numbers, Deuteronomy. These books make up the **Torah,** the Jews' most sacred book. [Judaism]

Five Ks Kes, Kangha, Kara, Kirpan and Kachera. Symbols which ordained Sikhs must wear. [Sikhism]

Gaia Consciousness a movement which stresses the importance of treating the planet earth as a living organism.

Grace God's undeserved love. Also the name for the Christian prayer of thanks at mealtimes. [Christianity]

Gunas the three qualities or characteristics which make up the material universe and which are found in humans: goodness, passion and dullness. [Hinduism]

Gurmukh living life according to the Gurus' way; God-centred. [Sikhism]

Hadith a narration containing the exact words spoken by the Prophet Muhammad. (See also **sunnah**) [Islam]

Halakhah 'a going'. Another name for Jewish law, so called because Jews think of keeping the commandments as 'going with God'; also spelt halachah. (See also **mitzvah**) [Judaism]

Harun the Arabic name for Aaron, brother of Musa (Moses); both prophets in Islam. [Islam]

Havdalah a ceremony performed at the end of Shabbat to say farewell to the day of rest. Havdalah requires wine, spices and a plaited candle. In the ceremony, Jews thank God for giving them the Sabbath and for distinguishing it from the other days of the week. [Judaism]

Humanism a view of the universe, and a way of life based on it, that is based on the evidence of the natural world and its evolution and not on belief in a supernatural power. It is therefore a naturalistic life stance that looks to human knowledge, experience and responsibility to solve the problems of this world.

Humanist a person whose personal philosophy is **Humanism**.

Icon a picture of Jesus, his mother Mary, or a saint, carefully painted onto wood. [Christianity]

Iman faith. In Islam this implies belief in Allah, his angels, his books, his messengers, Divine Destiny, the Day of Judgment and Life after Death. [Islam]

Isa Jesus. A prophet to Muslims. [Islam]

Isha literally night. The name given to the night prayer offered by Muslims after the sky has become completely dark. [Islam]

Isma'il Ishmael, son of Ibrahim (Abraham), both prophets to Muslims. [Islam]

Itikaf voluntary seclusion within the mosque (or home) during **Ramadan**. [Islam]

Jibril the angel Gabriel, who brought the Qur'an from Allah to the Prophet Muhammad **(PBUH)**. [Islam]

Jina an enlightened being. [Jainism]

Ka'bah the cube-like building at the centre of the Holy Mosque in Makkah. The first building dedicated to the worship of Allah. Rebuilt by Ibrahim and his son Isma'il and by the Prophet Muhammad **(PBUT)**. [Islam]

Kabbalah 'that which is received'; the Jewish mystical tradition. Kabbalah deals with such topics as God's relationship with the world, the nature of the soul and the purpose of creation. [Judaism]

Kufr disbelief. [Islam]

Laillha ilallah Arabic text, the first part of the Shahadah, meaning there is no god but Allah. [Islam]

Langar a meal served in a gurdwara; also the place where the meal is served. [Sikhism]

Lunar month the Muslim months begin with the sighting of each new moon. This means that most months are 29 days long but a few are 30. With 12 months this means that the lunar year is about 11 days shorter than the 365 day year based on the earth's movement about the sun. [Islam]

Madinah Madinatu'n-Nabi literally the City of the Prophet. The name given to Yathrib after the Prophet Muhammad **(PBUH)** migrated there. Situated approximately 650 kilometres north of Makkah in Saudi Arabia. [Islam]

Maghrib the evening prayer in Islam. Offered after sunset. [Islam]

Mahavira 'the Great Hero'. The name given to Vardhamana (599-527 BCE), the twenty-fourth and last pathfinder of Jainism. [Jainism]

Maimonides a popular term for Rabbi Moshe ben Maimon (1135-1204), one of the most influential Jewish philosophers and halakhic authorities. [Judaism]

Maitreya the name given to the historical Buddha who it is believed will live on earth in the future. [Buddhism]

Mala a rosary usually made of steel or other material, including cotton, wool, wood or seeds. [Sikhism, Buddhism and Hinduism]

Manmukh living life only for individual satisfaction, for self only. [Sikhism]

Mantra sacred words, prayer or a chant. [Hinduism]

Meditation the act of concentrating, for example on an object or thought [Buddhism, Christianity, Hinduism, Judaism and Sikhism]

Messiah the anointed one. [Christianity and Judaism]

Midrash rabbinic teachings, usually of a moral nature, set down not according to theme, but as they emerge from the verses and wording of the **Tenakh**, the Jewish bible. (See also **Mishnah**.) [Judaism]

Mikveh a pool of natural water (today, a pool of heated water joined to one of natural water), used for immersion. In ancient times, anyone wanting to visit the Temple would first immerse in a mikveh. Today, it is mainly used by women after menstruation and childbirth. [Judaism]

Mishnah rabbinic teachings (mainly Jewish law) set down in writing by Rabbi Judah the Prince in c. 200 CE. Unlike **midrash**, which follows the order of scripture, the contents of the Mishnah are arranged according to theme. [Judaism]

Mitzvah 'commandment'. One of the 613 commandments in the **Torah** covering every area of life. [Judaism]

Moksha release. Liberation from the cycle of birth, death and rebirth. [Hinduism]

Murti an icon or image; manifestation of a **deity**. [Sikhism]

Musa the prophet Moses. [Islam]

Nam Simran meditation. [Sikhism]

Om An alternative spelling for the sacred syllable (see **Aum**). [Hinduism]

Paranirvana a state of bliss beyond all possible return. The ultimate release from samsara, which can only happen at the time of death. [Buddhism]

PBUH Peace Be Upon Him. Used by Muslims when referring to a prophet. [Islam]

PBUT Peace Be Upon Them. Used by Muslims when referring to prophets. [Islam]

Perfections states of mind which have purified all delusions such as hatred and greed and have therefore become perfect. Enlightened beings have six perfections. [Buddhism]

Ramadan the ninth month of the Islamic calendar, during which Muslims fast during the hours of daylight. [Islam]

Renunciation the state of mind in which a being has totally shed any desire to achieve material benefits and wishes only for spiritual progress in life. [Buddhism]

Resurrection rising from the dead. Christians believe that Jesus was resurrected at the first Easter. [Christianity]

Sabbath see **Shabbat**. [Judaism]

Sahaj leading a balanced life of harmony between self, environment and prayer. [Sikhism]

Salah the Muslim prayer. [Islam]

Samsara 'flow', the Sanskrit word for the unsatisfactory nature of the cycle of life and death. [Buddhism and Hinduism]

Sewa voluntary selfless service. [Sikhism]

Shabbat the Sabbath. The holiest day of the week when Jews are required to cease all weekday activities and devote themselves to spiritual matters. Shabbat commences at sunset on Friday and ends Saturday night. It is generally celebrated as a family day. [Judaism]

Shabbos another pronunciation of **Shabbat**. [Judaism]

Shahadah the confession of faith made by Muslims. [Islam]

Sufism an Islamic movement with origins in the second century of Islam which has sought to develop the spiritual awareness of its members. [Islam]

Sunnah the practices of the Prophet Muhammad (PBUH) including his words, actions and silent approvals. These are taken as a model upon which Muslims base their lives. [Islam]

Tasbih a string of beads, either 33 or 99 which assists the Muslim in counting during dhikr. [Islam]

Tawaf walking around the **Ka'bah**, part of the rites of hajj. [Islam]

Tawhid belief in the oneness of Allah. [Islam]

Tenakh the Jewish bible; not a real word at all but a term made up from the initial letters **Torah**, Neviim (books of the prophets) and Ketuvim (holy writings). Sometimes spelt Tanakh or Tanach. [Judaism]

Tirtha ford, a place for 'crossing over' – from the physical to the spiritual. [Hinduism]

Torah 'instruction'. The Jews' holy book, which they regard as God's instructions for living a moral and spiritual life. In the synagogue, the Torah is read from a hand-written parchment scroll. Jews often use the term in an extended way to include the writings of the prophets as well as the teachings of the rabbis till the present day. [Judaism]

Waheguru 'Wonderful Lord'. [Sikhism]

World to come Judaism teaches that human history as we know it is not open-ended but that it will eventually reach its allotted span, after which it will be replaced with something more spiritual. That future age beyond the span of human history is known as 'the world to come'. It is also called 'the day that is eternally **Sabbath**'. [Judaism]

Yogi/yogini the male and female terms for those who practice spiritual activities such as yoga and meditation. [Buddhism]

Yom Kippur the Day of Atonement. The holiest day in the Jewish calendar when Jews fast for 25 hours and pray for forgiveness for their sins. It occurs in late September-early October. [Judaism]

Zakah a pillar of **Islam**, payment of a part of one's wealth to the poor and other groups named by the Qur'an. [Islam]

Zakat-ul-fitr donation given to the poor at the end of **Ramadan**. [Islam]

Zamzam a well near the **Ka'bah** in Makkah. Its discovery ended Hajar's search for water, a search which is commemorated during hajj. [Islam]

Index